MR. UNIVERSE

MR. UNIVERSE

AND OTHER PLAYS

BY JIM GRIMSLEY

ALGONQUIN BOOKS OF CHAPEL HILL   1998

Published by
ALGONQUIN BOOKS OF CHAPEL HILL
Post Office Box 2225
Chapel Hill, North Carolina 27515-2225

a division of
Workman Publishing
708 Broadway
New York, New York 10003

Printed in the United States of America.
Published simultaneously in Canada by Thomas Allen & Son Limited.
Design by Anne Winslow.

LIBRARY OF CONGRESS CATALOGING-IN-PUBLICATION DATA
Grimsley, Jim, 1955–
    Mr. Universe & other plays / by Jim Grimsley.
        p.   cm.
    ISBN 1-56512-202-X (hardcover).—ISBN 1-56512-211-9 (pbk.)
    PS3557.R4949M7   1998
    812'.54—dc21   98-10196
                                                                     CIP

10 9 8 7 6 5 4 3 2 1
First Edition

For Faye Allen and Del Hamilton

Contents

I would like to acknowledge support from the Fulton County Arts Council, the City of Atlanta Bureau of Cultural Affairs, the Georgia Council for the Arts, the Rockefeller Foundation, the National Endowment for the Arts, and the Mary Ellenberger Camp Foundation, at various times during the writing, development, and production of these plays. I have no way to express fully my deep indebtedness to Seven Stages, and to all the people who have worked there, for more than a decade of support for my work.

Introduction

The world, and in particular the world of writing, offers few torments as exquisite or pleasures as sweet as the opening night of a play. Here I have written all these words for people to say to one another, described all these pictures, sat through rehearsals, and suddenly here it is in front of me on a stage, all cleaned up, about to announce itself. A play that I have written is to be spoken and walked through, night after night, and tonight is the very first time.

Each play has its own terrors, and the creation and production of a script is an act unlike any other, borrowing from novel-writing, literature classes, the psychologist's couch, and the motivational seminar. A novelist can afford to be private and reclusive; a playwright may have tendencies in that direction, but sooner or later there will be a rehearsal or a party after a rehearsal or a performance or a question-and-answer session: sooner or later the nature of theater will drive the playwright public, at least for a while.

The publication of this book, collecting some of the plays I have written over the last decade and a half, is an opening of a different kind. I have been looking over the pages of these plays again, visiting them as if they were relatives I hadn't seen in a while, remembering the first time I saw the Muscle Man pull off his clothes in *Mr. Universe*, the first night I watched Pug Montreat shoot himself in the mouth in *Math and Aftermath*, the first time Eleanor stood in the window looking across the fields in *The Borderland,*

and Sol Heiffer's first walk across stage with the crucified lizard on her back in *The Lizard of Tarsus*.

To write a novel is a delicious siege; one camps in front of a story as though it were a city and waits. To write a play is like crossing a river by leaping from rock to rock; there are always those pauses, those moments of empty space, between the rocks. To publish a novel is a quiet process, at least as far as I have known it, with faxes and phone calls and thoughtful conversations, and parcels traded back and forth via overnight express. To produce a play is rarely a quiet business, with the fuss of meetings, the egos of artists and designers, the forced pressure of the short rehearsal. The two ways of writing provide a good tension, and each changes the other and makes it better.

But there is nothing I have known in fiction that can compare with sitting in a theater on the first night a play is performed, hearing spoken aloud the words that were delivered to the writer in silence. There is nothing like going back again and again and hearing how the language can change even when the words do not, how meaning can ripple across the space of the theater like something visible. A novelist cannot sit inside the reader's mind and feel the response the novel creates, but a playwright can sit with the audience and feel how they respond to the play.

The writing of a play or a book is a whole, and taking the process apart to examine it serves no purpose for the person who is doing the work. It is possible to make up a reason for writing or a theory of what makes a play, but in the end what matters is the play that gets made. The reason I make a play is so that I can sit there night after night and have the feeling of the words washing over me, of the scenes and voices out of my mind moving on the stage.

These plays share that need—to transform words into motion

in order to come to some moment of contemplation, in the midst of all that motion, that cannot itself be put into words or experienced in anything but silence. Here are four plays with puzzles inside them, with nothing neatly resolved or explained, which have already made the long journey to one stage or another. They are my attempt to draw some outline around the territory of mystery so that I myself might enter and others might follow if they so choose.

Jim Grimsley

MR. UNIVERSE

Romulus Linney, on *Mr. Universe*

The discovery of our common humanity in unlikely places makes for lively theater, but only as long as the humanity is as real as it is lively. False notes here quickly betray opportunistic sewer shock, not a procedure that holds up on a stage, where flesh and blood face flesh and blood, where honesty and truth as well as shock are mandatory. Otherwise, how do very strange beings placed before us have anything to do with our "normality"? We go to the theater to find ourselves in Shakespeare's universal mirror held up to nature, and find ourselves we must, no matter in what place or in what action or in what characters.

At the center of Jim Grimsley's *Mr. Universe* is a mute young bodybuilder covered with blood. Around him and his never-explained mystery circle, in various stages of emotional and sexual excitement, a decent drag queen, a vicious one, and a prostitute from whom God save old men. This takes place in New Orleans, which can often seem unreal, a Disneyland of Vice. Here is the real thing, populated by truthful citizens of its lower depths, those who hustle its streets after hours when tourists are safe in their hotels. That these vivid wrecks can be delightful as well as appalling, touching as well as murderous, that their concerns awake our own, about children, self-preservation, and love itself, is a testament to Jim Grimsley's refusal to judge them, to condescend to them, or finally, to exploit them.

The action of *Mr. Universe* is admirably clean and simple. Its world is simply as is. But the dialogue of the play is something else. Here, in what may seem by now the ordinary back-and-forth of gay chatter, lies the jewelry of the play. For what these people say to each other hits home. There is here a world of conflicting values, centering around such permanent matters as honor and betrayal, dignity and abasement, compassion and hatred, and the eternal essentials of drama, love and death. Loving and dying and speaking. You experience this in the exact and particular way these outlandish characters talk to each other, as much as in what they say. Line after line seems struck off from a living being, not a character in a play who must advance its action. Free from the fatal flaws of self-descriptive speeches, returning subjects, or long tales of the past, the people of *Mr. Universe* speak as we spoke to each other in our own past. As far as we may individually be from camp or bitchery, we hear them, and we understand their fear and rage and love, the basic emotions of life that drive them, and us. The unsolved mystery of the bloody bodybuilder becomes a sort of place, a safe thicket from which we can see amazing animals as they pass by. We have never met anything like them, not because they are so strange, but because they are so much like those elements of our own makeup we never acknowledge. The mirror is held up to nature, very peculiar but very truthful nature, and we see ourselves whether we like it or not. At the beginning of the play, we don't. At the end, we do. In between, a work of stage magic has shown us what we did not know we knew, never felt what was there to feel.

And we sense, in the anonymous author all playwrights must remain, lurking behind the different characters, a superior and unique artistic sensibility. Mr. Grimsley is a writer for many seasons. The poetic diction of his devastatingly brutal novel *Winter Birds* is an example of how much this writer can do, if we let him do it. His novels are now receiving the attention they deserve. Let us hope his plays will do the same. But here there is a problem.

Mr. Universe is challenging theater, especially for producers. It must be not just well acted, but brilliantly acted, or the underlying humanity will not emerge. This intense creation can easily play as nothing more than a sketch of violent sex life in New Orleans. Its stern delicacy and underlying fidelity to its world would be trivialized only too easily by a theater interested in immediate and obvious effect, which in this case would be camp. Think of the very best realistic actors you know, from both stage and screen, when you read this play—Al Pacino, for instance, or the young James Dean—and you can imagine something that would in my opinion, jump to a much different life on the stage than satire or lower depths despair. It would be life as it is, and it would be wonderful.

Jim Grimsley's characters are what let us hope God preserves us from, but we laugh and nod while we shudder. Keats was right. Beauty is truth, truth beauty, and Jim Grimsley got it right in *Mr. Universe.*

MR. UNIVERSE

Mr. Universe premiered at Seven Stages Theatre in Atlanta in August 1987, in a production directed by Steven Kent, featuring Mike Jones as the Saxophone Player, Rebecca Ranson as Juel Laurie, Faye Allen as the Police Woman, Del Hamilton as Vick, Tim Martin as Judy, Jeff Lewis as the Muscle Man, and Donna Biscoe as Katy Jume. Costumes were designed by Stephanie Kaskel, and composition and sound design were by Michael Keck.

The play was subsequently produced by Woodie King Jr. at New York's New Federal Theatre in March 1988, again directed by Steven Kent, with Nao Takeuchi as the Saxophone Player, Shami Chaikin as Juel Laurie, Vicki Hirsch as the Police Woman, Del Hamilton as Vick, Peter Toran as Judy, Charles Mandracchia as the Muscle Man, and Donna Biscoe as Katy Jume. Costumes were designed by Stephanie Kaskel; lighting, by Linda Essig; and set, by Steven Perry.

The song "Your Daddy" is an original composition by Jim Grimsley for *Mr. Universe*.

The SAXOPHONE PLAYER

JUEL LAURIE, a woman in her late forties or early fifties, widow of Vanice

A POLICE WOMAN

VICK, a man in his early forties

JUDY, a man in his early twenties

The MUSCLE MAN, a bodybuilder

KATY JUME, a woman in her late twenties or early thirties

SETTING

The play is set in 1979 in New Orleans.

ACT 1

SCENE 1:

> *Esplanade Avenue, a night in late spring.*
> *Lights rise on the* SAXOPHONE PLAYER, *who is rehearsing in the*
>   *cool night, playing traditional New Orleans jazz.*
> *Enter* JUEL LAURIE, *dragging a bag of garbage.*
> *The bag has a hole in it, and she trails garbage behind her.*
> *She stops once or twice to pick up the garbage she has dropped,*
>   *returning it to the bag but never quite comprehending that*
>   *the bag has a hole in it.*
> *Finally she reaches the garbage can and puts the bag in it.*
> *She walks away from it a few steps, then stands still, thinking.*
> *Enter* POLICE WOMAN, *who watches the* SAXOPHONE PLAYER
>   *and* JUEL LAURIE.
> JUEL LAURIE *returns to the garbage can, takes out the bag,*
>   *opens it.*

She begins to lay out the garbage neatly around her.

The SAXOPHONE PLAYER *lets the music soften and die away.*

Sits and begins to polish his horn, clean the mouthpiece.

Lights fade on him.

JUEL LAURIE *finishes arranging the garbage and speaks.*

JUEL LAURIE. I should've brought me some paper so I could do a list. I hate to throw this stuff away and tomorrow I won't even remember what it is. Looka this. (*Holds up an old shoe.*) I knew it. I knew. I never meant to throw this out. It ain't but one shoe but it's a good one. (*Smells it.*) Smells just like Vanice, Lord help me. Vanice, I says, your feet stink because you never wash from between your toes. I told him.

(*The* POLICE WOMAN *approaches.*)

POLICE WOMAN. Excuse me ma'am, what are you doing?

JUEL LAURIE. Oh God, did I do a crime?

POLICE WOMAN. You can't leave all this stuff laying around.

JUEL LAURIE. I was making a list. Are you going to put me under suspicion?

POLICE WOMAN. I just want you to clear up this mess, ma'am.

JUEL LAURIE. This is a good shoe.

POLICE WOMAN. Yes ma'am, you can keep the shoe.

JUEL LAURIE (*bagging up the garbage*). You ain't seen Vanice running around here have you? He left the house this morning without no belt on, and his pants so baggy they be all down his legs.

POLICE WOMAN. Is Vanice your husband?

JUEL LAURIE. Lord yes, everybody knows that. Everybody knows Vanice, he's got big feet. Why do you work for the police? Do you like crime?

POLICE WOMAN. No ma'am.

JUEL LAURIE. Has they been any good crime around here today?

POLICE WOMAN. Found a dead man in a motel over to the Faubourg. Don't know who he is.

JUEL LAURIE. Did he have a belt on?

POLICE WOMAN. Didn't have much of nothing on from what I hear.

JUEL LAURIE. Can't be Vanice then, he ain't never naked. (*Ties the bag closed and puts it in the garbage.*) I got to go fry some boloney. You want a piece?

POLICE WOMAN. No ma'am. You don't let no strangers in the house now.

> (*Exit* POLICE WOMAN.
>
> *Enter* VICK, *in high drag.*
>
> *He stays out of sight until the* POLICE WOMAN *is gone.*)

VICK (*to* JUEL LAURIE). What did she want with you, Mistress Laurie?

JUEL LAURIE. Hey Vick. That's a mighty nice dress you got on, did you go back to work at JuJu's?

VICK. No ma'am, I'm just going out. What did that policewoman want?

JUEL LAURIE. She got me under suspicion. She found a dead man in a motel, naked as God, over to the Faubourg.

VICK (*laughing*). She don't think you killed him, honey.

JUEL LAURIE. She might think I did, and Vanice ain't here to testify. Lord I need him so bad.

VICK. Mistress Laurie, now I've told you, you got to put him out of your mind, you can't bring him back.

JUEL LAURIE. The pohlice are coming back, you know that, they don't never come just once. She let me have my shoe but she's coming back for me.

VICK. Sweetheart come with me, come on. That's right. We got to get you back in your apartment right now.

JUEL LAURIE. I got to cook my supper. Fry some boloney.

VICK. Yes ma'am, you do.

JUEL LAURIE. Will you be home?

VICK. Judy and me are going out for a little while but we'll be back later, you can knock on the door when the light's on.

JUEL LAURIE. Katy ain't home. I know that. She out walking in a cheap dress, left her kitchen window wide open.

VICK. I know honey, I ain't seen Katy in a few days. But you'll be all right. Just keep the front door closed and come see me and Judy later when we get back.

> (*Enter* JUDY, *also in drag.*)

JUDY. What's wrong with her?

VICK. She came out on the street and got a little confused.

JUDY. I would not call that a little confused.

JUEL LAURIE (*to* VICK). Are you still taking up with him? (*Indicates* JUDY.)

VICK. Yes ma'am, Mistress Laurie, and Lord knows I don't know why. (*To* JUDY.) I'm just walking her back to her apartment, I'll be right back.

JUDY. You better be because I'm not waiting around, not long as it took me to get this garter belt right.

VICK. Oh hush, it won't hurt you to wait two minutes.

JUDY. I know it won't hurt me dear, but what about you, you're aging every second.

VICK. Kiss my ass.

> (*Exit* VICK *and* JUEL LAURIE.
>
> The SAXOPHONE PLAYER *has finished his instrument cleaning and stands, begins to play a slow, mournful blues—Judy's theme, "Your Daddy."*
>
> JUDY *struts up and down the stage, timing her sashay to the music.*

Enter VICK, *putting on lipstick.*

Music dies away.

The SAXOPHONE PLAYER *withdraws to his playing area;*
lights down on the SAXOPHONE PLAYER.)

VICK. Sweetheart what are you trying to do, make this month's
rent?

JUDY. You always get jealous because I have better legs than you do.
Don't you think you've put on enough lipstick by now?

VICK. Please don't flap your hand in my face. And who do you
think you are teaching me about makeup when I have worked
on the professional stage. You can't teach me anything about
being a woman, I have done it all.

JUDY. I bet you have. All at JuJu's Hideaway.

VICK. Your mama never worked any better place honey, not even
with real tits.

JUDY (*haughtily*). I do not want to talk about my mama if you
don't mind.

VICK. Are you ready to go? (*Takes a few steps.*)

JUDY. I am not interested in one bar up that street, I am tired of old
men and chicken.

VICK. Well I am not going to ruin my good gown walking up and
down the waterfront to find you a sailor.

JUDY. Why not?

VICK. You are completely out of your mind; the sailor never sailed
who would give you the time of day.

JUDY. But you promised.

VICK. Just exactly when did I promise to walk down to the waterfront and get myself killed?

JUDY. You said you thought it would be fun.

VICK. I said I thought it would be fun if we could fool them boys,
but we can't.

JUDY. All we ever do is go to the same old bar and drink the same old drink and talk to the same old men.

VICK. I am not having this discussion with you again.

JUDY. I want to have some fun Vick, please take me down to the river, please please. I'll be such a good girl you won't even know me. We'll just walk down there and walk back, we don't have to stay.

VICK. And you'll pick up some trash not fit to clean toilets and have him laying up in my apartment till I throw him out.

JUDY. You're jealous.

VICK. Sweetheart, when you get your own apartment you can sleep with every bum from here to Lake Charles.

JUDY. Please don't start at me Vick, you know I can't afford my own place, I still got to pay Maison Blanche for my alligator pumps.

VICK. Shut up whining about them shoes. Here comes a friend of mine.

> (*Enter* MUSCLE MAN, *whose large muscles are obvious even through his clothes.*
>
> *He walks tentatively, as if he were lost in the city.*
>
> *He stops some distance from the drag queens.*)

JUDY. You never knew anybody like that in your life.

VICK (*obviously stricken, not camp*). Did you ever . . . just look at that!

JUDY. I could peel him like a grape. Do you think he's one of us?

VICK. He's too butch.

JUDY. Well sweetheart, we're not all sissies. Though you'd never know it by the company we keep. (*Laughs at his own joke.*)

VICK. Don't cackle like a crow, he isn't paying the least attention to you.

JUDY. You mean he isn't paying any attention to you.

VICK. No he isn't. I didn't say he was.

JUDY. What's the matter honey, you falling in love?

VICK. Stop it, don't talk so loud.

JUDY. It's nothing to be embarrassed about dear, you can't help it. It's the Cinderella complex, it's a common thing for us girls. When you see a man like that you can't help dreaming he's Mister Right.

VICK. Shut up, I'm not dreaming anything.

JUDY. You really are upset aren't you?

VICK. Let's go.

JUDY. No, I think I just want to stand right here for a while and check out the street life.

VICK. Well you can stand here by yourself.

JUDY. You wouldn't dare leave me here by myself dressed like this.

VICK. Don't bet on it sweetheart.

JUDY. You wait a minute.

VICK. Life's too short dear. I don't have all night, and neither do you, I've seen you after midnight.

(*Exit* VICK.)

JUDY. You come back here. Vick!

VICK (*from offstage*). Why I can almost hear that sweet disco music.

JUDY (*exiting, looking back at the man*). Wait a minute. Wait for me, please wait.

SCENE 2:

Sounds rise: traffic noises, voices, a ship's horn, faint.
The lights lower till there is just one patch of light where the
MUSCLE MAN *is standing.*
The scene changes.

A stagehand drags off the garbage cans.

*Another clears away any other representation of the apartment
    building.*

The SAXOPHONE PLAYER *blows a few bars, drinks bourbon from
    a flask, blows a little more.*

The POLICE WOMAN *wanders through, exits.*

The SAXOPHONE PLAYER *descends, circles the* MUSCLE MAN,
    playing; exit SAXOPHONE PLAYER.

Traffic noise fades; a pulsing beat begins.

The MUSCLE MAN *takes off his clothes, slowly stripping to a pair
    of posing trunks.*

He simply stands still with his clothes onstage around him.

*As music grows slowly louder and the lights change, he paints
    himself with streaks of red paint, like blood, as if he were
    creating wounds.*

*The blood can come from anywhere, and its source need not be
    hidden.*

Enter KATY JUME, *in a tight cocktail dress.*

KATY. So I told him to get his goddamn hands off me. Told him he
    looked worse than shit in a pot. Touch my titties one more
    time and I will cut his hands off. Make me sick. I don't even
    want to know who he is or what his name is. Shit-ass mother-
    fucker keep your hands off my drink too. Drag your scrawny
    ass out of here. Leave me money for a drink and get out. Yes
    sir, I said leave me money for a drink or I'll pull every hair out
    of your head. I said every one and watch me do it. I don't care
    who hears me. Don't talk that bullshit to me, I'll snatch the
    false teeth out of your mouth. Yellow-tooth motherfucker. I
    wish I could embarrass you to death.

    (*Sees the* MUSCLE MAN *sitting on the grass of the neutral
        ground.*)

What are you looking at?

(*The* MUSCLE MAN *goes on watching her without moving or speaking.*)

Get up off the ground staring at me. Answer me when I talk to you. I don't care how good you look, you don't sit on the ground staring at me. I'll beat your head in. I'll be responsible for your death, do you hear me? Get up from there. Get up I said.

(*The* MUSCLE MAN *slowly stands.*)

You got blood all over you.

(*Enter* JUDY *and* VICK.

VICK *is holding his wig in his hand.*)

VICK. I'd never believe we'd be on our way home at this time of night.

JUDY. Would you shut the fuck up?

VICK. I don't want to rub salt in the wound, darling, but you have just made a complete and total fool of yourself in world-record time.

JUDY. If you say one more word I will kill you.

VICK. Never has one queen so completely humiliated herself in public. I doubt Pinky will ever let you back in the door.

JUDY. If I had a gun I'd blow your brains out right here on the street. Not that it would make that much of a mess. What happened tonight is not that big a deal.

VICK. View the wreckage dear. You ran your poor boyfriend right off the planet. You made a shambles of my dress. I smell like dog piss. God only knows what has been on that floor besides me.

(*They stop near* KATY *and the* MUSCLE MAN.)

JUDY. Honey, has he been yours for long or are you just now sinking your teeth in?

KATY. You better back away from me, Judy.

JUDY. I beg your pardon, I didn't mean to intrude. We saw this young gentleman earlier, didn't we Vick?

VICK (*to the* MUSCLE MAN). It looks like you've been in a fight.

KATY. I found him sitting on the ground. He won't say nothing. He's got blood all over him.

VICK. You poor baby, what happened? (*Pause; no response.*) Did somebody get after you? Did somebody do this to you? (*Pause; no response.*) There's something wrong with him.

JUDY. Not from where I'm standing.

VICK. Shut up Judy. (*To the* MUSCLE MAN.) Are you all right? Do you need some help? (*The* MUSCLE MAN *does not answer but makes eye contact with* VICK *for a beat.*) I think maybe we ought to take him home. Do you want to come home with me?

KATY. He don't act like he knows what you're saying.

VICK. Do you want to come home with me? So I can clean you up? Don't be scared, you poor thing. I don't think he knows how to talk.

JUDY. That's fine with me, he'll never need to say a word.

VICK. Come on sweetheart, I won't let this mean thing hurt you. (*The* MUSCLE MAN *moves to* VICK'*s side.*) You want to come up for a while, Katy?

KATY. I might as well. I lost my keys again.

VICK. Well you can sleep on the couch tonight and call the landlord tomorrow. Are those his clothes?

KATY. I'll get them.

JUDY. This is wonderful. He looks just like a Ken doll. He can sleep with me tonight.

VICK. Judy, this man is hurt. Leave him alone.

JUDY. Who named you Florence Nightingale? You can't tell me what to do.

VICK. You heard me.

JUDY. You are not going to keep this man all to yourself Vick darling.

> (JUDY *tries to touch the* MUSCLE MAN.
>
> VICK *slaps his hand.*)

VICK. You listen to me. I am dead serious. You behave.

> (JUDY *withdraws, angry.*)

VICK (*to* MUSCLE MAN). Come on with me. That's right, come this way. You coming, Katy?

KATY. I'm right behind you. Lord, these are some nasty clothes.

> (*Exit* VICK, KATY, *and the* MUSCLE MAN.
>
> JUDY *remains behind, furious.*
>
> *Lights dim as he removes his wig.*
>
> *The* SAXOPHONE PLAYER *plays softly offstage.*
>
> JUDY *smears his makeup with his hands till it is*
>
> > *grotesque.*
>
> *Sashays offstage behind the others.*)

SCENE 3:

> VICK's *apartment. Living room and kitchen.*
>
> *Enter* MUSCLE MAN, *into the living room, carrying his clothes in*
>
> > *his hand.*
>
> *He sits on a low stool or chair under low light and is wearing*
>
> > *the posing trunks as before.*
>
> *Enter* JUDY *and* KATY, *into the kitchen.*
>
> JUDY *is still wearing the dress.*
>
> *They should enter a few moments after the* MUSCLE MAN *sits.*
>
> *At the end of* VICK's *speech, lights rise in the kitchen and* KATY
>
> > *is heard.*

KATY. So I told him I would cut him if he ever showed his face around that restaurant again. I wouldn't even use a meat knife on him, just an old potato knife, and I'd carve him up so good I might as well cook him, there wouldn't be any use to do nothing else with him. Motherfucker turn so white, Lord you should have seen it child. His little old cock just wither right away. I told him he rather not ever lay his hands on me, nor show me anything so puny. You know I told him.

JUDY. Try this.

KATY. That's got too much bourbon for him.

JUDY. You think so?

KATY. Yeah, he been beat up, you don't want to knock him out. Give that to me and make him another one.

> (*Enter* VICK, *with a basin of water, towels, and materials for bandages for cleaning the* MUSCLE MAN.
>
> *He makes as many trips as necessary to prepare for his first-aid ministrations.*
>
> *He has washed his face quickly and is wearing either the dress or a dressing gown, somehow maternal.*
>
> *A wig is lying in the living room in a conspicuous place.*
>
> *He bathes the* MUSCLE MAN, *cleans the wounds, and applies bandages.*)

JUDY. Well how much should I put in?

KATY. Hold it up and jiggle it a little. Just a little. Yeah, that's right. Now pour something else on it, and you got a drink.

JUDY. Let me see what I can find to mix with it. (*Opens cabinet.*) Look at this mess. We don't ever have nothing fit to eat. Oh, here's some tomato paste!

KATY. You don't want none of that.

JUDY. It would be gummy, wouldn't it. And I guess we don't want any canned baby lima beans and we don't want any cornbread mix, puffy and fluffy and all, and we don't want any pre-sweetened fruitade and we don't want any instant ice tea or powdered nonfat instant dry milk. (*Moves to refrigerator.*) No sprouts, God I hate sprouts, no tofu, Jell-O or white Minute rice, no we don't want to mix our bourbon with any of that stuff. Did you see this cake? I made it myself.

VICK (*as he cleans the wounds*). Hold still now, I'll be real gentle but it might sting a little. That's right, hold still, that's real good. Nobody's going to hurt you. Vick's going to take good care of you, bandage you up real nice and get you something to eat and put you to bed, and then tomorrow we'll find out who you are and where you live and get you home all safe and sound.

> (*Enter* KATY, *into the living room, with drinks for* VICK *and the* MUSCLE MAN.
>
> JUDY *stays in the kitchen long enough to freshen his drink aggressively.*
>
> KATY *gives a drink to the* MUSCLE MAN, *who simply holds it as if he doesn't know what it is.*)

KATY. Judy is about gone tonight.

VICK. Tell me some news sweetheart. Did she tell you what happened in the bar tonight? Down in Pink Lilly's Valley? Judy pulled a knife on a married man, with a wife and everything. I didn't even know Judy carried a knife, and me walking the streets with her as pretty as you please.

KATY. I been knowing she carried a knife.

VICK. I tell you what's the truth, I don't know what I'm going to do. She acts crazier every day.

KATY. Her mama act exactly like her.

VICK. Don't even mention that woman to me. Do you know she's back in town and has not even bothered to call? She disappears for months without telling anybody where she is and then comes back without a word. I saw her dancing the other day at that place on Bourbon Street. I haven't even told Judy yet.

KATY. She tell me she don't want no queer boy for no son, walking around the French Quarters in a wig and a dress.

VICK. She's just jealous because he's got a better figure than she does.

KATY. She have got fat. I don't know why people pay her to take off her clothes. (*Pause.*) Judy would have been better off staying with his gramama than coming down here anyway. This city ain't no good for nobody.

(*Silence.*)

VICK. I'm beginning to think he's selling drugs out of that bedroom.

KATY. You got to be kidding.

VICK. He's getting money from somewhere. (*Pause.*) I don't think he cares what he does anymore. Let me tell you. In the bar tonight you never saw such a flame. This girl was on. You could not keep her off the tabletops and you could not keep her skirt down over her knees. She was gone on something, no telling what.

KATY. Probably two or three things, knowing Judy.

VICK. Well then this man comes up and she is just all over him, I mean she's got her hands all down in his pockets. This nice-looking man. Then Judy grabs at something and holds it up, and Lord, do you know she had pulled that man's wedding ring out of his pocket and she was whooping and waving it around and hooting all over the bar. With that poor man just standing there.

KATY. You sure it won't a cock ring.

VICK. Lord I hope not, it was mighty little. Anyway, I felt sorry for that man. Then he got mad and went after Judy, tried to tear off her dress. Judy pulled a knife on him and like to cut his throat. I had to grab the knife from her. Then the man knocked me down in the beer and ruined one of my good gowns. I don't know if that man ever got his ring back. Judy and me were thrown out of the bar, and we're lucky they didn't call the cops. Girl was gone with a blade in her hand. (*Pause; looks at the drinks* KATY *is holding.*) Did you bring that drink for me or is it an extra for you?

KATY. Oh no, it's yours. I was just admiring your buddy here. He sure does look good when he clean.

VICK. Yes he does.

KATY. Look on that poor baby's back. You got cut real bad, sweet man?

VICK. The cuts aren't all that deep. When they're not bleeding you can hardly see them at all. It's like he fell on glass or something. He's got some bruises too.

KATY. That's going to swell up ugly.

VICK. Yes it is. Who would do something like this to such a pretty baby?

KATY. Lots of folks. I got a boyfriend would do it just so he could laugh about it when he finish. He ain't my main boyfriend but he good.

VICK. I ought to take him to Charity but I don't feel like messing with that emergency room tonight.

KATY. Maybe it was a pack of them little boys that dance in the street when them blue-hair ladies throw money. Pack of them mean suckers, them little devils, carrying knives and every-thing else.

VICK. He don't look like he was cut with a knife.

KATY. You think that's clean enough?

VICK. I need to wash it with peroxide, but I wonder if he'll hold still.

KATY. He looks right calm to me.

VICK. You think you can be still while I wash your back with some stuff that smells funny?

>   (*The* MUSCLE MAN *simply watches* VICK.)

VICK. I want you to keep still, do you think you can?

>   (*The* MUSCLE MAN *looks straight ahead.*)

VICK. That's a good man. That's just what I want.

KATY. I think he must like you.

VICK. Wouldn't that be nice.

KATY. He do look good. He look like this man I knew in Chicago, only this man had great big hands with real big bones.

VICK. This man's hands aren't so small.

KATY. They ain't big like my man's hands was, when I was in Chicago. Big old knobby fingers. I love them old fingers, old nasty thing.

VICK. Honey you can make anything sound nasty, you ought to be ashamed of yourself.

KATY. I sure don't know why I would bother.

>   (VICK *is dressing the* MUSCLE MAN *in a pair of loose pants.*)

VICK. Let me help you. Don't listen to this nasty lady who talks so mean, she really ain't mean at all, I been knowing her for a long time.

KATY. Don't you believe it either sweet legs, I cut you as quick as I look at you.

VICK. Why do you want to talk like that to my big baby doll, you know you never cut nobody in your life.

KATY (*to the* MUSCLE MAN). I will cut you, or your mama or your baby sister, or your wife in front of your eyes, or your boyfriend if you got a boyfriend, or your motherfucking newborn child. (*To* VICK.) Look at him! He trip me out.

VICK. He doesn't understand a word you're saying.

KATY. He like a great big doll baby. Stand up doll baby. Stand up.

VICK. Stand up, she won't hurt you.

(*The* MUSCLE MAN *stands.*)

KATY. How come you stand up when this hag tell you to?

VICK. I am not a hag.

KATY. Hey big boy, why don't you like me? I'm a real girl. This here thing, she ain't even got tits. I got tits. Why don't you come over here to me. (*Pause; no response.*) He don't want to come nowhere near me. He a queer is what it is. He a faggot just like you. He don't like to smell no real woman.

VICK. I don't think he's gay.

KATY. Hey girl, just look at him. He got them sweet eyes, he look at you all gooney, just like a faggot. He got big faggot muscles and gooney faggot eyes and he stand on one hip just like a faggot, and he look in the mirror at his body just like a faggot. Excuse me, I don't mean to make you mad when I use that word.

VICK. It takes a lot more than that to bother me baby, or else I'd be right out of business. But like I said, I been spotting faggots for years and I don't think this man is one.

KATY. Wouldn't it be nice if he was.

VICK. What do you care what he is?

KATY. I like to see you with somebody nice. Not like this trash you got living with you now. This man here might be real good for you.

VICK. Don't get me started daydreaming Katy.

KATY. But that might be what he came here for. It might be the angels sent this man for you.

VICK. Stop making fun of me.

KATY. I'm not playing, I'm serious. Ever since I been knowing you I wanted you to get you some big strong man who treat you right. This man here look like he might be real good.

VICK. He is sweet looking isn't he?

KATY. He got sweet eyes, like this man I met in the bar. This salesman. Fellow with stringy blond hair and big ugly gold rings on his fingers, them kind turns your skin green. That man wasn't sweet though. He sold Christmas ornaments, can you believe that? I told him I thought that was a kid's job to sell that shit. He have a kid's face too, come up putting his hand on me, I don't care if he did sell Christmas ornaments.

VICK. What did he do?

KATY. Reach all up in my dress like he know what was there, till I about snatch his fingers off. I'm not lying. I liked to knock him down with my whiskey.

VICK. Had you been talking to him or did he reach up your dress first thing?

KATY. I been talking to him, but that don't mean he can grab my thigh like it was a chicken leg. How would you like it if some fool ass grab on you when you minding your own self having a conversation? I told him he better not ever do that to me again. Don't nobody touch Katy unless she want to be touch. That man got right sweet then. I told him he act like a kid. Just like my baby brother. When my baby brother grab my titty, I slap him. Then I feel right sorry for this man after I told him off so bad, so I ask him to show me his Christmas ornaments. But he say he didn't have his case with him. I ask him where it was and he say in the hotel.

VICK. Did he take you there? Girl you nasty thing, to his hotel?

KATY. I didn't mind, I had me a good time looking at that fool bulbs what he had. Lord I wished I had me some I could wear for Christmas earrings. He never put his hand on my leg again either.

VICK. You mean you went with this man to his hotel room and he already tried to squeeze you in a bar but he didn't even touch you in the room?

KATY. That's what I said. Maybe he touch me once but that was all. We ought to get something to eat. I want some ice cream. Something sweet.

VICK. We have some cake. Chocolate banana. Miss Thing made it. Betty Crocker in there washing off her makeup.

KATY. I know, I saw it. I didn't know she could cook. I rather have a pizza.

VICK. Pizza's not sweet.

KATY. I rather have a pizza but I want something sweet too. Why do you keep your cake in the refrigerator? Last time I look in there it like to knock me out.

VICK. Shut up, don't let this baby hear you talking about my housekeeping like that.

KATY. I mean it. If it still smell like that in there I won't even mess with no cake. (*Heads for the kitchen.*)

VICK. Save me a piece.

KATY (*pauses*). Girl did I tell you I was hired to do me a commercial?

Yes ma'am just like that Brooke Shields. On TV. Don't look at me like I'm crazy, I'm not lying. (*Exits to the kitchen but continues talking.*) I'm going to be the Mammarismo Girl. You know what that is? The Mammarismo Exercise Bra? Lord they gave me one and I thought it would pinch me to death. Got these big springs across it. I told them I would take the job but I be damn if I wear one of them ugly bras except on the commercial. You ought to get you one, maybe it would develop you some breast.

VICK. I don't want no breast I can't drop in a drawer.

KATY. You mean you don't want a fine set of these here like I have?

VICK. Noo sweetheart, what would I do with them when I'm waiting tables?

KATY. Anyway, I be standing in front of the camera and I have on this big bra and the tops of my boobs is all pooched out, and I pucker my lips and say, "Mammarismo, the Exercise Bra: The Bra with the Squeeze that Pleases." Can you hear me? "Mammarismo, the Exercise Bra: The Bra with the Squeeze that Pleases." And I got a scarf around my neck and the wind just blowing and blowing from this big nasty fan they got set up. I believe I'll get me some dark glasses too. I be standing there with nothing on but these dark glasses and a big bra. You never seen anything like it. I will be more fine than fine.

VICK. Don't get that cake on my floor.

KATY. You don't hold no truck with me honey, this floor is already filthy. If you stand still too long the roaches be crawling up your legs.

VICK. When do you do this commercial?

KATY. What commercial? Oh yeah, I don't know. They call sometime tomorrow or the next day. I hope my phone ain't cut off. I make five hundred dollars in one day if you can believe it.

And I get my hair done free. They gave me one of them free bras too and I'm going to fasten it to the wall and use it to hold up my bookshelf where I keep my magazines. I read *Star Weekly.* You ever read that? Girl, you can find out everything. I read about this woman had a monkey for a baby because she got the wrong sperm. Some kind of sperm or something. Can you believe that? She was getting artificial disseminated and had a monkey. I say it serve her right. Nobody going to stick a needle in my sweet cake, no no no. I'm not having a monkey for a baby for nobody, I don't care how smart the monkey is. Bad enough having a baby for a baby.

VICK. Do you have a baby?

KATY. I got a little girl, she live with her gramama. She six. She don't even hardly know me.

VICK. I got a little son.

KATY. What fool do you think you're talking to?

VICK. No, I really do. His name is William Zachry. He lives with his mama. He's twelve this September.

KATY. You really are serious.

VICK. I was married for about three years. Yes ma'am. Back when I was a real man.

KATY. What did you do with your wife to get that baby?

VICK. What do you think I did with her?

KATY. You mean you did like a man does?

VICK. Katy sweetheart, I'm not missing any parts. It's not all that complicated.

KATY. But I didn't think people like you could do that stuff with a woman.

VICK. A monkey could do it if he set his mind to it. If he could get over how funny looking you was.

KATY. Was your wife funny looking?

VICK. No, she was pretty. This blond hair like you would kill for, and big thick lips and she was pink color all over, like a little lollipop. And my son, Lord you should see him, pretty as a girl and sings like one of the angels. They got him in the church choir. One time when I went to see him he sang a solo on "Near to the Heart of God," all by himself, and the old ladies in the church were looking at him like it was the rapture. He favors his mama more than me.

KATY. Did you like her?

VICK. I loved her, I really did. I don't think I was fooling myself. But I liked men too. So we got divorced after she found out.

KATY. How did she find out?

VICK. She caught me in bed with one of her cousins.

KATY. Lord, I believe I would have choked you to death.

VICK. She came at me with a knife. Her mama tried to call the police but I got out of the house. We're friends now, I send her money and everything. She come to see me when I was doing drag at JuJu's, she thought it was funny.

KATY. What make you like men?

VICK. I don't know. I just do.

KATY. If my men ever tell me they like men better than me I cut they little head off right there. I mean it. I could kill somebody for tricking me like that.

VICK. Why would it be a trick? I won't tricking anybody.

KATY. You must be crazy. You don't think your wife feel trick, sitting there home with that youngun and you out here spending more money on clothes than she does.

VICK. It wasn't like a trick, it was like I didn't know any better.

(JUDY *calls from offstage.*)

JUDY. Come in here and help me unhook this gown.

KATY. And you carrying on with something like that. Your little child come to see you?

VICK. Sometimes. (*To* JUDY.) I'll be there in a minute.

KATY. You take him out to the bars with you?

VICK. Fuck off Katy, what do you think?

(VICK *starts to exit, angry.*)

KATY. I don't think nothing. Hey Vick. (VICK *stops, hearing unaccustomed tenderness in her tone.*) Hey Vick I didn't mean nothing by it, I was just asking questions. When my little girl grows up I'll take her out.

VICK. It's not the same thing.

KATY. I know. You got a picture of your little boy?

VICK. Somewhere.

KATY. Bring it back with you.

(*Exit* VICK.)

KATY. I should have known he had a little baby. You know? All this time I been knowing him and he never said nothing about it. Got a little boy twelve years old, and him running around the streets in a dress whooping and hollering and carrying on. (*Laughs.*) Vick on a woman, can you imagine it? Vick on a woman just humping away, and got a baby and never said nothing. (*To* MUSCLE MAN.) I bet he's a good daddy to his child. I bet he feed that child and write letters to him and talk on the phone, and I bet he say happy birthday to that child and send him Santa Claus at Christmas. Vick would be a good daddy. If he didn't have this trash living with him like he got now. Me and Vick, we friends. Yeah. I bet you don't believe it do you? Vick, he likes me, he really do. We been friends a long time, ever since I move downstairs. He look good too, if he didn't put on them women clothes all the time. Don't you think he look good? Come on baby, if you can understand Vick you can understand me. Don't you like Vick? Don't you wish you could stay here with him? I do. I think you ought to. You could be like his little child. He never had anybody real nice like you, he only had tramps like that Judy. I'm serious. He would take real good care of you. That's what you want, ain't it? Don't look at me all blank like these boys, you don't fool me. You're here because you want something, just like me. You a faggot too, just like I said. You like to wear dresses and strut that stuff on the street, I know. Look here . . .

> (KATY *finds* VICK's *wig, which has been left on stage; she puts it on the* MUSCLE MAN.)

Now you look right. You look like you are.

> (*The* MUSCLE MAN *removes the wig.*)

Put it back. You heard me, put that back on your head. Put it on your head I told you. Are you stupid? Can't you hear?

> (*Enter* JUDY.)

JUDY. What are you fussing about in here?

KATY. This man is stupid. He sits there like he don't know anything, all swoll up like a ape.

JUDY. What is he doing with my wig?

KATY. That's Vick's wig.

JUDY. Well what is he doing with it?

KATY. He had it on his head and then he pull it off.

JUDY. On his head? He put it there? By himself? Wonderful, maybe there's hope. How did he look?

KATY. Like a big Girl Scout.

> (JUDY *puts the wig on the* MUSCLE MAN.)

JUDY. Oooh yes, this is the look of the future. Marilyn Monroe with biceps.

(*The* MUSCLE MAN *pulls off the wig again.*
Holds it up in his hand and shakes it as if he does not
know what it is.)

KATY. He can't make up his mind.

JUDY. Doing drag is a big step in a young man's life, you can't just jump right into it, you have to take it a little at a time. Lucky for him I'm here to provide counseling and guidance.

KATY. He almost got titties already.

JUDY. Those are not titties, dear. That is called development, pectoral definition. With me it's a definite requirement.

(JUDY *replaces the wig on the* MUSCLE MAN.
The MUSCLE MAN *throws the wig across the room.*)

JUDY. Now what did you do that for? (*Gets the wig.*) This is a perfectly good one hundred percent human hair wig and there is no reason to treat it worse than a dust rag.

KATY. Maybe he don't want it on his head.

JUDY. But he looks so sweet in it. I know! He's mad because he knows the wig doesn't look right unless you're wearing makeup.

KATY. Girl you crazy.

JUDY. Where's some makeup? What you got in your purse?

KATY. Are you serious?

JUDY. Of course I am. We have got to do this boy up right. What do you have?

KATY (*looks in her purse*). Here. Some red lipstick and some eye shadow and some blush.

JUDY. You be like my helper now, you hold that stuff till I ask for it and then you give it to me. I'm going to have my hands full.

KATY. You can cool believe that.

JUDY. Now you be real calm young fellow. We'll fix you right up, yes sir. Don't worry about a thing. I been turning out pretty girls for years. May I have the blush, sister Katy?

KATY. There it is, take it.

JUDY. You're supposed to slap it in my hand like I was a surgeon.

KATY. Take the goddamn mess and stop clowning.

>   (JUDY *puts blush on the* MUSCLE MAN, *who sits still for it*
>   *but looks suspicious.*)

JUDY. Whatever you do don't laugh. Eye shadow.

KATY. What?

JUDY. Give me the eye shadow.

>   (KATY *gives* JUDY *the eye shadow.*
>
>   JUDY *attempts to apply the eye shadow.*
>
>   *The* MUSCLE MAN *draws away from* JUDY*'s hands.*)

JUDY. Look it won't hurt you. See? It's like medicine for your face.

>   (JUDY *applies the eyeshadow unevenly, hurriedly.*
>
>   *The* MUSCLE MAN *sits still but is becoming angry.*)

KATY. What do you want to do this to this man for?

JUDY. Lipstick.

>   (KATY *gives* JUDY *the lipstick.*
>
>   *At the sight of the red lipstick emerging from the tube,*
>   *the* MUSCLE MAN *backs away.*
>
>   JUDY *follows him with the lipstick.*)

JUDY. Hold still now, we're almost done.

>   (JUDY *manages to smear lipstick on his mouth.*)

JUDY. My God. Throw me the wig. Throw it to me, quick.

>   (KATY *throws* JUDY *the wig.*
>
>   *Enter* VICK, *with a tray of food, as* JUDY *puts the wig on*
>   *the* MUSCLE MAN.)

VICK. What are you doing?

JUDY. Playing dress-up.

VICK. Get that mess off of him.

JUDY. But he looks so cute.

VICK. You heard me, get that away from him and stop teasing him.

JUDY. Well my, aren't our maternal instincts just popping out?

> (*The* MUSCLE MAN *is agitated but does not move, as if*
> *the wig has paralyzed him.*
> VICK *sets down the tray.*)

VICK. You can't leave anything alone, can you. You always got to
be messing with people. Any fool can see there's something
wrong with this man, he does not need you after him.

JUDY. Don't look like there's anything wrong with him to me.

VICK. Shut the fuck up. You are disgusting to me sometimes.

> (VICK *removes the wig.*
> *The* MUSCLE MAN *begins rubbing his mouth, smearing*
> *the lipstick.*)

VICK. Calm down, calm down, I'll wash it off.

> (*The* MUSCLE MAN *strips and flexes his arms as if prov-*
> *ing his manhood.*
> *Flexes them again.*
> *Flexes them one at a time, almost in a frenzy.*)

VICK. Calm down.

> (*The* MUSCLE MAN *becomes calm.*)

JUDY. You make me sick.

VICK. Come over here.

> (*The* MUSCLE MAN *follows* VICK *to a window seat.*)

KATY. I swear this man would do whatever you told him.

JUDY. Why don't you sit down in his lap. Why don't you just crawl
all over him since he likes you so much.

VICK. Did it ever occur to you he might be scared? He's been wandering around God knows how long, got beat up, can't talk
and Lord knows what else. We don't even know who he is.

JUDY. I'm not interested in his identity problems, I wanted to improve his social life.

VICK. All you know how to do is try to be funny. (*To the* MUSCLE MAN.) Don't worry, I won't let them put the wig on you anymore.

KATY. I didn't put any wig on anybody, you leave me out of this.

JUDY. This girl is gone on this man, this young woman has lost her mind, Looney Tunes. She has met the man of her dreams.

VICK. What the fuck do you know about my dreams?

JUDY. Look at how you are behaving, you can't keep your hands off him, you're completely out of control.

VICK. I have not laid a hand on this man except to put on his bandages and wash off his blood. You're jealous because he likes me and I won't let you play with him like he was a puppy.

JUDY. Here is this handsome young man in our apartment who will do anything she tells him to do and suddenly she is the Mother Superior of Esplanade.

VICK. I wish you knew how sick you sound.

JUDY. What's wrong with the way I sound? This is a gift from God, this doesn't happen every day. Don't be a prude. You can't look a gift horse in the mouth as they say, not when it's a horse like this.

(JUDY *goes toward the* MUSCLE MAN.)

VICK. Leave him alone.

JUDY. You must be joking.

VICK. If you lay a hand on him I will kick your puny ass.

JUDY. I'm over twenty-one dear and unless I miss my guess so is he.

VICK. I said stay the fuck away from him.

JUDY. Get out of my way.

VICK. I'll break your fucking face.

JUDY. The fuck you will.

> (*They come as close to having a physical fight as possible*
> *without committing to it.*
>
> *Finally* JUDY *breaks up laughing.*)

JUDY. This doesn't make any sense.

VICK. You'll think it's real funny when I put your suitcases on the street.

JUDY. Don't start that shit.

VICK. I'm not playing with you, I've had about all I can stand.

JUDY. All you can stand? Bitch, you don't even want to get me started.

VICK. I mean it. You can drag your mealy ass into your bedroom and stuff every feather boa you've got in a shopping bag and get out. Get out. Then see how long it takes you to find somebody else to pay your bills and feed you and drag your drunk ass home from Bourbon Street.

JUDY. I pay my rent goddamnit.

VICK. The hell you do. Don't act up for Katy's benefit, I have told her all about you. Strut around here like you're some kind of princess and strew your clothes all over hell, leave your nasty dishes for me to clean up and drag your common-ass boyfriends across my rug, and tell me what you will do and you won't do, hell! I'll pack your shitty dresses myself.

JUDY. I could understand if we were fighting over which one of us is going to get him. But I don't see why at least one of us can't fuck him since he's here.

KATY. You don't have you any babies of your own, do you Judy?

JUDY. What?

KATY. You don't have any children do you? You ain't never took care of nothing but you.

JUDY. What in the fuck are you talking about? I ain't said nothing about a baby. I just want to know what in the hell we brought this man home for if we're going to treat him like a vestal virgin.

VICK (*calmer*). He was hurt and we brought him home to clean him up. He's scared and we're not going to bother him. Tomorrow we're going to find out who he is and where he belongs.

JUDY. This is just like what you did to me in the bar. Every time I want to have any fun.

(*Knock on the door.*)

KATY (*whispering*). If that's for me I ain't here.

JUDY. Well Miss Vain, who would come up here looking for your ass?

KATY. You heard me. You haven't seen me all night.

JUDY. Where are you going?

KATY. To your bathroom to pee and don't you say a word about it.

VICK. What are you whispering for?

(*Knock on the door.*)

JUDY. I'm coming, I'm coming, keep your skirt on.

KATY. You do like I said or you'll be sorry.

(*Exit* KATY.

JUDY *opens the door.*

Enter POLICE WOMAN.)

JUDY. Excuse me.

POLICE WOMAN (*showing her badge*). I'm looking for your downstairs neighbor Katy Jume.

JUDY. I haven't seen Katy for a while. I guess you already tried her apartment.

POLICE WOMAN. Yes I did. You folks live around here long?

JUDY. I've been here a few months. My roommate has been here several years. Isn't that right?

VICK. Yes.

POLICE WOMAN. How long have you known Katy Jume?

VICK. A couple of years. Is something wrong?

POLICE WOMAN. Does he live here too?

VICK. He's a friend of mine from out of town. He can't talk.

POLICE WOMAN. Can't talk?

VICK. I think it was because of a shock when he was a little boy.

POLICE WOMAN. I don't want to hear all that. You see Katy Jume, you tell her I'm looking for her, and I'm going to find her. You get this man some clothes on.

JUDY. I beg your pardon.

POLICE WOMAN. Don't beg honey.

(*Exit* POLICE WOMAN.)

VICK. What was that all about?

JUDY. I don't know but I intend to find out.

(*Exit* JUDY *and* VICK.

The SAXOPHONE PLAYER *plays softly.*

The VOICES FROM OUTSIDE *are heard.*

The MUSCLE MAN *crosses to the wig, lifts it, poses with it in his hand, places it on his head, and smiles.*)

THE VOICES FROM OUTSIDE. You know I heard that yeah Revondela do you have any chewing gum in your pocketbook Lord girl I done tore my panty hose who are you to talk to me like that you shit-head motherfucker walk on down to Bourbon Street with your sorry ass think you so fine, so fine I can walk like that, I can string myself all over the sidewalk like a strumpet, you know what I'm talking about, child go on out of here, stop looking at that man, he going to come over here and drag you down in the bushes. He look fine. He really do.

END OF ACT 1

ACT 2

SCENE 4:

> JUDY's *bedroom.*
>
> *Lights rise on the picture of Judy Garland.*
>
> *Piles of clothes are everywhere.*
>
> *Enter* KATY.
>
> *Music is playing softly as if from another room.*
>
> *The sound of water running.*
>
> KATY *pulls off her dress, drops it on the floor, walks on it, kicks it*
>   *aside.*
>
> *From her purse she pulls out a knife, cleans it.*
>
> *The music grows louder.*
>
> *She dances a sultry dance with the knife.*
>
> *Anoints herself in perfume.*
>
> *Wraps herself in a feather boa lying on the floor.*
>
> *Enter* JUDY.

JUDY. What are you doing in my bedroom? I been looking all over the house for you.

KATY. I'm standing here admiring your picture.

JUDY. Where's your dress?

KATY. Over there. I got hot.

JUDY. You know who that was at the door, don't you?

KATY. Yeah, it was the Avon lady bringing me my makeup I ordered.

JUDY. It was the police. This hateful-acting woman. She was asking about you. She wanted to know how long you had been living here and if we had seen you.

KATY. Peoples all over town be curious about me, it don't worry me at all.

JUDY. Katy, why are the police looking for you?

KATY. Look at these nasty clothes on the floor. You got more dresses than the Queen of Sheba. Don't you ever clean your room?

JUDY. Have you been talking to the police about things you aren't supposed to talk about?

KATY. If you mean them nasty little drugs of yours, no I have not said anything about them.

JUDY. You better not have if you know what's good for you.

KATY. I shake in my shoes when you talk like that. I really do.

JUDY. Honey if you run to the police on me there will be bloodshed and hair flying.

KATY. Grow up girl. The cops have a lot bigger asses than yours to worry about.

JUDY. You better be telling me the truth.

KATY. Don't shoot this shit to me. You ain't bought nobody, sweetheart. You don't know me that good. You can wave all the shit you want to in my face but I know it ain't mine. Drag me out some of that stuff.

JUDY. Do what?

KATY. You heard what I said. Get it out.

JUDY. You've got a lot of nerve coming in my bedroom and ordering me around.

KATY. As much money as I've made for you, you can spare me a little taste. Come on now, my nerves is all wore out.

> (JUDY *finds a metal or wooden chest in which there are
> many Baggies and syringes—drug paraphernalia.*
> KATY *reaches for the box.*
> JUDY *backs away.*)

JUDY. First you tell me what did the police lady want.

KATY. She didn't want nothing man, she was lonely. Give me that box.

JUDY. Talk to me first.

KATY. She was probably just a dyke who follow me home.

JUDY. When was the last time a dyke followed you home?

KATY. They follow me around all the time. Give me that baggie.

JUDY. What did the policewoman want, Katy dear?

KATY. She didn't want nothing, get out of my face.

JUDY. You tell me or you don't even get to smell of this good stuff.

KATY. Girl, you are making it so I just have to pull a knife on you.
            (*Moves toward her purse.*)

JUDY (*reaching for his own knife*). You touch a knife and you'll get more of a fight than you know what to do with.

KATY. Ain't nobody scared of you.

JUDY. Ain't nobody scared of you either baby. Now act like you got some sense. We are in this together. I got a right to know why you're messing with a policewoman.

KATY. I ain't messing with nobody.

JUDY. All right, you're not messing with her, she's messing with you. She said she wanted to ask you some questions.

KATY. I know what she said. I was with this salesman in his hotel room over in the Faubourg and he had a heart attack. He fell over dead and I had to go downtown.

JUDY. Where did you go downtown?

KATY. To the police farm honey, to big blue heaven. That's right, me myself. Sitting in this grimy room with this big fat-belly policeman grinding his jaw like he was trying to wear his teeth out. I had to tell them all about this man heart attack why he died. He was just this man I pick up in the bar.

JUDY. He had a heart attack while you were fucking?

KATY. We hadn't even done anything, he barely got his clothes off. He was kind of old, fluffy-ass motherfucker.

JUDY. If you already talked to the police why do they need to ask you more questions?

KATY. I don't know. They couldn't find any driver license on him and they didn't know who he was. Maybe they have some pictures for me to look at. I think he might have been some kind of murderer. The police act like they know all about him.

JUDY. You're kidding. Who did he kill?

KATY. A whole bunch of people over in Slidell.

JUDY. God, I've got to start reading the newspaper sometime. (*Starts to give* KATY *the baggie, then pauses.*) Listen, I want you to help me with something.

KATY. What?

JUDY. Help me with that muscle man in there.

KATY. What do you want to do to that poor little innocent baby?

JUDY. That baby is not little, sweetheart, and when I get through with him he won't be innocent either.

KATY. If you mess with that man, Vick will kill you dead.

JUDY. Vick can act like some old lady if he wants to, I'm going to put to use what the Good Lord has provided.

KATY. I don't think you understand what I'm trying to tell you. Vick already threw a fit all over you, he will kill you if you mess with that man.

JUDY. I know that. That's why I want you to keep him busy. Get him real upset about the police. You know Mother Vick, he'll sit right down and forget about everything else.

KATY. You ain't getting me in between all this.

JUDY. Katy honey, I'm your mother. Do what mother tells you. All I need is ten or fifteen minutes.

KATY. What the hell are you going to do in fifteen minutes but scare the poor child to death?

JUDY. You don't worry about him for a minute. Once I get him to the bedroom, he'll relax just fine, and so will Vick.

KATY. You are absolutely crazy.

JUDY. I know Vick, honey. He's not a fool. Once he sees that me and that man are going to fuck, he'll leave us alone.

KATY. No you don't know Vick, and you don't know that man either one.

JUDY. Stop arguing and do like I said, for your sweet sister who gives you candy and takes care of you.

KATY. Why do you have to mess with this? That man and Vick are getting along just fine. You got a new boyfriend every week, you don't need to steal from Vick.

JUDY. That man don't want Vick.

KATY. Sure look like he does to me. I don't know what he want but he sure want something.

JUDY. You're dreaming girl. Face facts. Vick is old news. Now all I want you to do is tell Vick about the police and get him out of here for a little while, just a little while.

KATY. This ain't right.

JUDY. Don't talk that right shit to me.

KATY. I said this don't feel right. That man already been beat up and you want to get all over him with yourself. I think you better lay back and take a good long look. You hurt that man and Vick will put your bags on the street, and there will go the best setup your sorry ass has ever had.

JUDY (*as if he has heard nothing*). I'm counting on you, Katy sister, don't let me down.

KATY. I'ma tell you something. I am up to the roots of my hair with being sister to you. Don't call me that.

JUDY (*giving* KATY *the baggie*). Just take your medicine into the bathroom darling, you'll be much calmer about the whole thing when you're loaded.

KATY. You are nothing but trash just like the bitch that brung you into the world.

JUDY. Let's don't talk about Mother.

KATY. You know I saw that sorry-ass strumpet the other day, and I thought to myself how lucky you was that you ain't like she is, but I was wrong. You are low as the rug. If I had a child like you I would drown it like it was a dog.

JUDY. You ain't seen Mama, you are a lie. She ain't even in town.

KATY. Oh no honey, she back. She stripping at the Harum Scarum every night, her titties flopping every which a-way. Yeah, I saw her. I told her you said hello and happy Mother's Day.

JUDY. You utter goddamn bitch.

KATY. You can't name me nothing I ain't already been named, baby, it just roll right off my back. But let me tell you something. Don't act like that bitch tonight. Just as sure as I'm standing here, you fuck with Vick and this man and you will pay.

> (*Exit* KATY.
>
> *The* SAXOPHONE PLAYER *plays raucous, almost terrifying striptease music.*
>
> JUDY *picks up his clothes, handling the dresses carefully.*
>
> *Enter* MUSCLE MAN, *onto another part of the stage. He seats himself cross-legged.*
>
> JUDY *continues to clean his room, then pauses, standing by the telephone.*
>
> *The* MUSCLE MAN *pulls the bandages off his back.*
>
> *During the speech that follows, he paints himself with blood, as before, while the* SAXOPHONE PLAYER *continues to play, softly enough that* JUDY *can be heard.*)

JUDY (*picking up the phone and dialing*). Hello. Get me Ruby. Yeah, it's me. Yeah, I'm fine. Yeah look, get Ruby, okay? (*Waits for a long time.*) Hello Ruby girl. Why yes darling, it's really me. Well I'm just tickled to hear your voice. You know you are my main woman. That's right. You do have the money? Good for you. But believe it or not I didn't call about that. I have some news, darling. Yes, it's paradise. I have crystal. Yes ma'am, pure as the driven snow. Well the price is up. I don't quote price on the phone sweet child, what kind of tacky creature do you take me for? Don't worry, I can cut you a deal. I want a favor. Just a little one. Don't ask any questions. In about fifteen minutes I want you to call the police. The police. Downtown, that's right. You know Katy Jume? Tell the police you saw her coming into this building. Tell them you were walking by here. Well, walk by here then, I don't give a fuck. You do what I told you and I'll front you the crystal and charge you half price. You don't have to give them your name. Tell them you saw her coming in here. Don't answer any questions, tell them and hang up. Do it because you love me. Listen to me. Listen. If the police don't show up looking for the bitch, the whole deal is off. You got me? You can shoot up the desert sands for all I care. All right? Remember, wait fifteen or twenty minutes, like I said. Talk to you later. I'll call you. Yeah, I got the stuff right here. You're just a doll. (*Pause.*) Don't push your luck, I'll deliver. Night-night.

(*Exit* JUDY.)

SCENE 5:

(*Enter* VICK, *into the living room, where the* MUSCLE MAN *is sitting.*)

VICK. Baby, you've pulled off your bandages, you're bloody all over again.

> (*The* MUSCLE MAN *stands.*
>
> VICK *takes the bandages, wipes the blood.*
>
> *Enter* KATY.)

KATY. What's wrong with him now?

VICK. He pulled off the bandages and got the bleeding started again. Get me a towel.

> (*Exit* KATY.)

VICK. What am I going to do with you? I already got one child in this apartment.

> (*The* MUSCLE MAN *contemplates* VICK *carefully, then flexes his arms.*)

VICK. Yes I know, you have nice big muscles.

> (*The* MUSCLE MAN *continues to flex.*
>
> VICK *begins to touch one of the* MUSCLE MAN'*s biceps, then withdraws.*)

VICK. Put your arms down. Put them down, that's right. They're real pretty. They really are. But I don't need a show right now.

> (*The* MUSCLE MAN *paces as if disturbed.*)

VICK. What's wrong?

> (*The* MUSCLE MAN *will not hold still for* VICK *or look at him.*
>
> *Enter* KATY, *with a basin, cloth, and towels.*)

KATY. What's wrong with him?

VICK. I don't know. I think he's mad at me. He was showing off his muscles and I wouldn't touch him.

KATY. Why not? Are you crazy?

VICK. I don't know, I just couldn't. I didn't want to think about him like that.

KATY. Like what?

VICK. Like somebody I could touch. Like somebody who might want me to touch him.

KATY. Sound to me like that's what he want.

(*The* MUSCLE MAN *allows* VICK *to touch him now.*
VICK *begins to clean him and put on the bandages again.*
This continues during the scene that follows.
The effect should be that the MUSCLE MAN *and* VICK *are reading each other's minds.*)

VICK. I don't know what he wants. But I wonder. (*Pause.*) Did Judy find you? Did he tell you a policewoman was here looking for you?

KATY. Yes, he told me all about it.

VICK. What did she want?

KATY. I don't know.

VICK. What do you mean you don't know?

KATY. Vick, mind your own business. I don't want to talk about it.

(*A knock at the door—different, lighter than the* POLICE WOMAN's.)

VICK. Oh Lord, they're back. What do you want me to do?

(*Knocking continues.*)

KATY. Open the damn door, I don't give a shit.

VICK. You sure?

KATY. You can't act like you ain't at home, they can hear us talking.

(VICK *opens the door; enter* JUEL LAURIE.)

VICK. God knows, Mistress Laurie, you scared us half to death.

JUEL LAURIE. Oh Vick. I climbed them stairs, I ain't got breath. Lord. (*Pause.*) You said come up if your light was on.

VICK. Yes ma'am, I sure did.

JUEL LAURIE. Well, bad things is happening out there tonight. I keep hearing Vanice. Like he was in the hall. And the rats is back in the walls. All behind the toilet. Scratching like. I can't get no peace when I go in there. I put out poison but it don't do no good.

VICK (*to* KATY, *who has stepped to the doorway*). It's Mistress Laurie from downstairs.

KATY. Hey Juel Laurie.

JUEL LAURIE. Vanice said the pohlice looking for you girl.

KATY. You can't be listening to what Vanice tell you, he long gone from this world.

JUEL LAURIE. Vanice said how it was all on the news about you.

KATY. What was on the news?

JUEL LAURIE. The news was on when I left. River near up to the levee. All kinds of murder. Rats so bad you can't hear nothing. I had beans for supper, with ham. They is all off in the walls, you can't shoot 'em with a gun.

VICK. What was on the news, Mistress Laurie?

JUEL LAURIE (*to* KATY). It was something I wanted to tell you sweetheart, it might rain. Weatherman said it won't and he ain't never right.

VICK. Juel Laurie, did the police really come by your apartment or are you remembering the one you talked to this evening on the street?

JUEL LAURIE. No, it was after that. The pohlicewoman come by my house while the water was on. Anyway Vanice says the pohlice is after Katy Jume from downstairs what has the blue kitchen curtains blowing all out the window from the fan. Says the pohlice want to put her on the news big-time. Says Vanice. They fount a dead man in a motel, I was in the kitchen washing my hair. With the water running you can't hear a thing.

VICK. What time did they come?

JUEL LAURIE. Between *Twilight Zone* and *The Avengers.*

VICK. That was about the same time the woman was here.

JUEL LAURIE. I don't have no flashlight in my house.

VICK. What do you need a flashlight for, honey?

JUEL LAURIE. You can't see in the dark without no flashlight. That woman in the uniform looking for you, she'll find you too.

KATY. Do you see the future or do you just run your mouth?

VICK. Leave her alone, Katy, she can't help it.

JUEL LAURIE. That woman in the uniform coming to seize you, child. Take you down to the jail house and lock you in the room with the crazy woman and the dogs. (JUEL LAURIE *sees the* MUSCLE MAN, *crosses to him.*) Who is this here? Do you live here boy?

VICK. He can't talk, Mistress Laurie.

JUEL LAURIE. He can't?

VICK. No ma'am.

JUEL LAURIE. Why not?

VICK. I don't know.

JUEL LAURIE. What happened to him to get all those Band-Aids on him?

VICK. I think somebody beat him up.

JUEL LAURIE. Every time I turn around you took up with somebody else. Where is that other boy who used to live here?

VICK. He still does.

> (JUEL LAURIE *walks around the* MUSCLE MAN, *inspecting him.*
>
> *After a pause, the* MUSCLE MAN *stands, walks around* JUEL LAURIE, *inspecting her.*)

JUEL LAURIE. Hope you get your eyes full. Looking at somebody. (*To* VICK.) How did he get to be shaped all like that?

VICK. I guess he did a lot of exercises.

JUEL LAURIE. He looks like Vanice did when he was in the navy. I like this man, you art to keep him and get rid of that prissy one.

VICK. Juel Laurie, you got to finish what you started to talk about.

JUEL LAURIE. What was that?

VICK. The policewoman coming to see you.

JUEL LAURIE. But I told you everything I know. She's coming back for Katy Jume. She's watching your front door and the lights in your house. She's in the whole neighborhood visiting all your friends. She's coming back for you. She got a surprise.

VICK. I believe I hear Vanice calling you.

JUEL LAURIE. Vanice is in the bathtub reading *True Detective* magazine.

VICK. I believe he wants you to come home.

JUEL LAURIE (*to* MUSCLE MAN). Do you have a flashlight I can borrow?

VICK (*as if she has been speaking to him*). No ma'am. All I got is candles.

JUEL LAURIE. You can't kill rats with no candle. We got a flashlight but the batteries is dead on it. I ain't bought no new ones because we still got toilet paper. Vanice is calling me, ain't he?

VICK. Yes ma'am, he is.

JUEL LAURIE. Katy, honey, your kitchen window is open and the curtains is blowing all out of it.

KATY. I don't think it's going to rain right now, Juel Laurie.

JUEL LAURIE. Don't worry sugar, Vanice didn't tell the pohlice nothing. He was smart. He said he hadn't seen you and didn't know nothing about where you were. You got to treat your neighbors like your kin.

VICK (*leading* JUEL LAURIE *to the door*). Good night Juel Laurie.

JUEL LAURIE. I believe I'll make some grape Kool-Aid when I get home. Good night Mr. Muscle.

(*Exit* JUEL LAURIE.)

KATY. She said they're watching my house.

VICK. She doesn't know anything.

KATY. I need a clean dress. I ain't been home in three days.

VICK. You lied to me, didn't you? You didn't lose your apartment key. You were just afraid to go home because of the police.

KATY. I was a fool to come here at all.

VICK. Tell me why the police want to talk to you.

KATY. I don't know why.

VICK. Tell me the truth, Katy.

KATY. I might have seen something.

VICK. Why don't you play straight with me for five minutes.

KATY. I told you, I might have been someplace where something happened. Someplace where I was tonight. People always be getting killed around here, you can't worry about it. You just got to accept it.

VICK. Did somebody get killed where you were? Answer me.

KATY. Which place? I been a little bit of everywhere tonight, it has been one hellacious day.

VICK. I'm going to ask you one more time. Where were you that the police want to know about?

KATY. In bed with this two-bit pimp in Gentilly.

VICK. I can't ever tell when you're lying and when you're telling the truth.

KATY. Well this is the truth, honey. I was in bed with this pimp name Wienie Rod, and we was laying up in his trailer in a empty lot in Gentilly, and come a knock on the door. Wienie Rod walk over there in his pajama bottoms and a shotgun blast right through the door and tear his head clean off. By the time I got to him whoever it was with the shotgun had gone and there was Wienie Rod laying in a pool of blood with his head blowed off. I got right out of there. I went off and had me some breakfast.

VICK. You lying whore.

KATY. Who you calling a lie?

VICK. What happened when that salesman took you up to his hotel room?

>   (*A beat of silence.*
>
>   KATY *watches* VICK.)

VICK. Would you tell me what happened, please?

>   (*Enter* JUDY.)

JUDY. What is this, true confessions time?

KATY. As a matter of fact it was a private conversation. But since you're here you might as well know.

JUDY. Oh, is this about that woman who was here, that darling policewoman? You already told me about that.

KATY. I know what I told you.

JUDY. So this is an even truer true confession.

VICK. Could you please shut up?

JUDY. Miss Girlfriend to Miss Girlfriend, station to station.

KATY. Judy, I am going to cut up what you don't shut up.

VICK. Don't pay any attention to her.

JUDY. That's right, treat me like the mosquitoes and the flies.

KATY. Girl, you are high.

VICK. Tell me what happened, Katy.

KATY. Nothing happened.

VICK. The police aren't after you because nothing happened. They want to talk to you about that man, don't they?

KATY. What man? I know lots of mens.

VICK. You know what man. That salesman in the bar. The one who grabbed on you, the one who sold Christmas tree bulbs.

KATY. Oh yeah, old sweet-bottom. What do the police want to talk to me about him for? Come on, you been reading my mind, do it some more.

VICK. You said you went with him to the Faubourg.

KATY. That's right, I did.

VICK. The police told Juel Laurie . . . (*Hesitates, visibly decides to change the subject.*) Fuck it, forget I asked you anything.

KATY. No baby, you don't get off that easy. You want to act so concern, go ahead. Tell me what you think happened with that man.

VICK (*after a pause*). I think he's dead.

KATY. I can't hear you.

VICK. He's dead. He died.

KATY. Well Lord help me. How did he get dead?

VICK. I don't know.

KATY. You lie. You think I killed him.

JUDY. Vick's been watching too many police shows on TV.

KATY (*to* VICK). You really think I could kill somebody.

VICK. I don't know what I think.

KATY. You another lie. You think I could kill somebody, don't you?

VICK. Yes.

JUDY. Well Katy girl I guess now you know who your friends are.

> (KATY *laughs in such a way that it becomes plain* VICK *is right.*)

KATY. You should have seen that man, Judy, he was a trip. Greasy fucker. Think he can have me easy. Took me up to his hotel room and serve me cheap vodka on crush ice. Talk nasty in my ear about what he want to do, and then take my clothes off with his fat hands, and then show me a picture of his wife. Can you believe that? I don't know why. He was just drunk and one minute he was all over me and the next minute he was feeling bad and want to show me his wife. This nice-looking woman with good hair and smiling all kind of a nice smile. And him laying there on that hotel bed with the sheet pulled up over his fat belly, and looking all ugly with his teeth yellow from cigarettes. Waiting for me. I told him to put his pictures away and he did, and I thought it would be all right, but then he start to touch me and kiss on me and tell me how she don't treat him right, and all about how she can't even cook breakfast in the morning without breaking the yolk on the egg, when he so fat he don't need to eat another egg forever in his whole life. I got mad. I don't know why. I couldn't stand to look at him and I couldn't stand for him to touch me and I tried to get away but he was grabbing onto me, and I just got madder and madder.

JUDY. You told me he had a heart attack.

KATY. That's right, he did. I attack his heart myself. That was all last night. I got out of there and I been wandering around ever since.

VICK. Katy.

KATY. Don't say nothing. Because I'm not sorry. No sir, not one little bit. To tell you the truth I don't feel nothing at all.

VICK. But why?

KATY. I told you I don't know. It's done now and I can't take it back. It felt good to stick a knife up between his ribs. Men always sticking something in me, I wondered how it felt.

(*Enter* JUEL LAURIE, *onto another part of the stage, as if she is passing by in the hall outside.*)

JUEL LAURIE. Vanice. Vanice honey, are you out here? Vanice, supper is ready and I can't find you nowhere, I been looking all day.

JUDY. There she goes again.

JUEL LAURIE. I cooked a ham like you like. With the can cherries on it. You can make you some good sandwiches, Vanice baby. And we got baby lima beans and hot rolls. Vanice you got to change your socks, they all clean. Vanice, where are you, please answer me.

KATY. I hate it when she hollers like that.

VICK. She's upset tonight.

JUDY. That man been dead long enough she ought to know it by now.

JUEL LAURIE. Vanice, the saxophone man is down by the No Parking Anytime. We can go down and listen to him. He got the big gold horn, he'll play like you want. Where are you baby? I miss you. I ain't seen you all day.

KATY. Please go make her shut up.

VICK. She'll calm down in a minute, just sit still honey.

JUEL LAURIE. If you don't come back soon I'll be gone. That's right. Vanice, the pohlice looking for me, they think I killed somebody. The pohlice came talking to me, wanting to know where you were. You're the only one who can save me, they gone back after the big guns and the dogs. I need you so bad. You know it? You ain't no good. Do you hear me? You ain't no good for leaving me.

> (*Exit* JUEL LAURIE, *mumbling.*
>
> *For a time there is silence in the apartment.*
>
> JUDY *wanders to the window, sipping bourbon, smoking a cigarette if the actor smokes.*
>
> KATY *paces.*

The MUSCLE MAN *goes to* VICK, *who checks his bandages.*)

VICK. This is driving me crazy, I can't stand it. Give me the key to your apartment.

KATY. What for?

VICK. I'm going to get you a dress. Then I'm going to check the back door to see if there's anybody watching the courtyard. The police might not even know to watch there.

KATY. You must be crazy.

VICK. I can't just wait here.

KATY. You start helping me and they'll lock you up right along with me.

VICK. Sweetheart, they will never know. You are not just going to sit here waiting for them to arrest you because you killed some fat motherfucker from out of town. Give me your key.

KATY. Hell, I'll go down there.

VICK. No you won't. You're going to wait right here till I get back. Don't argue with me.

KATY. The key's in my purse.

JUDY (*gleeful that* VICK *is leaving*). Your purse is still in my room, Katy sweetheart. I'll go get it.

(*Exit* JUDY.)

VICK. I'm sick to my stomach all of a sudden. (*Goes to window.*) All you can smell is rain rot and garbage.

KATY. Can you see the police?

VICK. Not from here. I can see the saxophone man though, right where Juel Laurie said.

(*Enter* JUDY, *with* KATY's *purse and dress.*)

JUDY (*giving* KATY *the purse*). Here you are.

(KATY *searches for the key.*)

VICK (*to* MUSCLE MAN). I'll only be gone for a minute, I'll be right back.

JUDY. He looks tired, poor baby. Why don't I put him to bed in your room while you're gone? Then you can sleep with me tonight.

VICK. Are you serious?

JUDY. Vick, I am not a monster. I don't want to hurt this man any more than you do.

VICK. Well . . .

JUDY. Vick, please let me do something nice. I'll just tuck him in real pretty and by the time you get Katy all fixed up, he'll be asleep for the night.

VICK. That sounds sweet. All right. (*Gets the key from* KATY.) I'll be right back. Is there anything else you want?

KATY. Just bring me my red cocktail dress you gave me for my birthday.

VICK. How am I going to see that dress in the dark?

KATY. It glows, honey. You'll find it.

          (VICK *moves toward the exit.*

          The MUSCLE MAN *follows.*)

VICK. No, you can't come with me. I'll be back in a little bit.

KATY. That's sweet. He don't want you to go.

VICK. I'll be back in a minute. You let them put you to bed, all right?

JUDY. Aunt Katy and Aunt Judy will fix you right up.

KATY (*to* VICK). Don't let no spook get you. I thought I saw old man Vanice myself the other day.

          (*Exit* VICK.)

JUDY (*to* KATY). Poor baby. You need to calm down. (*Approaches her.*) Come on sweetheart, let me take you back to my room.

KATY. Get the fuck away from me. I can't stand you when you try to act nice.

JUDY. But I want to give you a little something to settle your nerves. Killing people is hard on a girl, you probably worked up quite an appetite.

KATY. You are sick.

JUDY. You mean you don't want any more of my candy?

KATY. You know better than that.

JUDY. Well I tell you what. You just go get you some. You know where it is. And take you a little bit for the road, you probably need it.

KATY. Are you serious?

JUDY. Of course.

KATY. You're going to let me in that box without hanging all over my shoulder?

JUDY. Katy dear, you are my friend. Friends trust each other. Besides, I promised Vick I would put this poor man to bed.

KATY. Oh, I get it now—

JUDY. No no no, you've got it all wrong. I'm going to do just exactly like I said, I'm going to put this man to bed and I'm not going to bother him one little bit.

KATY. You must think I'm a fool.

JUDY. I'm telling you the truth. I did a lot of thinking about what you said. I don't want to end up like my mother, keeping company with trash for the rest of my life. She threw away everything that ever did her any good. I don't want to do that. Vick is good to me and I'm going to start being good to him. So don't worry. I wouldn't hurt this man for all the muscles in the world. I'm going to take him into Vick's room and put him to bed and turn out the lights and leave him alone. I might even sing him a lullaby.

KATY (*wanting to believe him*). I hope for your sake you're telling the truth.

JUDY. I am. You can believe it. Now go on back to my room and look in my box.

(*Exit* KATY.)

JUDY (*calling after her*). Now don't take everything I got.

> (JUDY *turns to the* MUSCLE MAN, *walks slowly around him in a wide circle.*
>
> *The* SAXOPHONE PLAYER *plays* JUDY*'s theme, low.*)

JUDY. You think she really killed somebody? Do you? Come on, answer me. I know you can talk. Do you think Katy looks like a killer? She looks really hot in that slip, don't she? Yeah, you like that stuff. I can tell. The police are coming; did you figure that out yet? They'll probably drag you and her off both, don't you think? I mean, Katy killed this man. And you look suspicious too.

> (*The* MUSCLE MAN *moves toward the door.*
>
> JUDY *intercepts him.*)

JUDY. Where do you think you're going? Vick's not out there. Vick's not coming back. The police will be in Katy's apartment any minute, just hundreds and hundreds of them. He won't be coming back for a long time. He'd probably go downtown with Miss Katy anyway. He's so good. You can count on Vick, yes sir. Vick will take good care of Miss Katy. And you and me will stay right here.

> (JUDY *approaches the* MUSCLE MAN *slowly.*
>
> *The* MUSCLE MAN *withdraws.*)

JUDY. You can understand me, can't you? Yes you can. Don't run away. I just want to put you to bed. I can make you feel real good. Make you relax. I just want to take you back to Vick's room and put you to bed. And maybe get to know you a little.

> (JUDY *continues to approach throughout.*

The MUSCLE MAN *continues to retreat.*

JUDY *is surprisingly anxious that the* MUSCLE MAN
should believe he is sincere.)

JUDY. Why are you afraid of me? Why do you let that bitch Vick put his hands on you but you won't let me?

(JUDY *manages to corner the* MUSCLE MAN.

The MUSCLE MAN *pushes him violently away.*)

JUDY. If you would just let me try I could be okay. There's nobody here but you and me. You know? You don't have to pretend anymore. This is what you came here for, isn't it?

(JUDY *and the* MUSCLE MAN *are some distance apart.*

The MUSCLE MAN *peels off his shirt in slow motion,
strips to his posing trunks.*

JUDY *freezes, watching.*

The MUSCLE MAN *poses as the light changes.*

Eerie music plays, as if they were in some strange dimension.

The MUSCLE MAN *does a smooth, polished posing rou-
tine, both standing and kneeling poses.*

*He does the double biceps, spreads his lats, shows off
pectoral striation, thigh flexion, curved triceps, and
flaring deltoids.*

JUDY *watches for a long time and then approaches.*

The MUSCLE MAN *pushes* JUDY *away contemptuously
and continues to pose.*

JUDY *approaches again and is pushed away again.*)

JUDY. I've done this before, I'm sick of it. You can't just stand there, you can't just wait. You have to come to me. You have to want me too. (*Any anger here dissolves and becomes pleading.*) If you would try. Please. I can be okay, I really can. Please. Let me touch you, once.

(JUDY *approaches the* MUSCLE MAN, *who coolly slaps
     him and pushes him away.*

JUDY *goes off, anger building till he cannot contain it.*

*He destroys the apartment, completely wild, ripping pa-
     pers, magazines, and old clothes, throwing things,
     breaking things, absolutely out of control.*

The MUSCLE MAN *stands serenely, as if he had expected
     this reaction.*)

JUDY (*when he is finally calm*). Somebody is making all this up. You
     are, aren't you? You're making all this up while I'm standing
     here. Look at me. Look at me goddamn you. (*Pulls a knife.*)

     (*Enter* KATY.

     She stands at the side of the stage, watching.

     JUDY *does not notice her.*)

JUDY. Look at me. I'm here. I'm pretty. I am pretty. You can't just
     stand there, I'll kill you. Do you hear me? Answer me, I know
     you can talk. I'll kill you.

KATY. Judy girl, put that knife away.

JUDY. Fuck you. Fuck you and fuck him too. I am pretty, I am, I
     am. I'm as pretty as he ever was. But you can't tell him that, oh
     no. He's so holy. He can't even see you. Oh God. I can't do
     nothing with him, I can't even touch him. I could never reach
     him if I live forever.

KATY. Baby you're high.

JUDY. No, it's him. You know what I mean. It's him, it's just me and
     this man and we're stuck here, forever and ever and ever, oh
     goddamn everything.

     (JUDY *rushes the* MUSCLE MAN *a final time.*

     In the struggle that follows, JUDY *is stabbed with his own
          knife.*

The movement ends in an embrace, and JUDY, *in dying,*
slides toward the floor, tearing away the MUSCLE
MAN's *bandages.)*

Silence.

The MUSCLE MAN *kneels over* JUDY, *touches the wound,*
tries to move the body.

When it will not move, he backs away.

KATY *walks slowly toward* JUDY, *watching the* MUSCLE
MAN.

She kneels, hesitates, then picks up the knife.

She grips the knife as if she had killed JUDY.

She and the MUSCLE MAN *watch each other.*

Enter VICK *with red cocktail dress and red shoes.)*

VICK. Katy, some police cars just pulled up out front, Juel Laurie is
going to let us know what they do. (*Stops.*) What is Judy doing
down there? (*Kneels.*) Judy. Judy what's wrong?

KATY. She's dead.

(VICK *simply looks at* JUDY.

He finds the MUSCLE MAN's *bandages in* JUDY's *hands,*
picks them up, looks from the MUSCLE MAN *to*
KATY.)

VICK. What happened? (*Waits; no answer.*) Katy, tell me what happened.

KATY (*lifting the knife*). This happened.

(*Enter* JUEL LAURIE, *without knocking.*)

JUEL LAURIE. They're here sweeties. They got you surrounded, better come out with your hands up.

KATY. Where are they?

JUEL LAURIE. Down under the big crack in the plaster with the water
stain like Jesus' face, Vanice is on the landing keeping watch.

KATY. Are they coming up here?

JUEL LAURIE. Vanice says not yet. Don't worry. He won't sing out loud, they won't see him. Vanice can be real quiet when he wants to. I told you they would come back. Katy Jume is here and they know it, they say they got a call. They see through walls and open windows without their hands. Better hide, better transport you away on one of them beams, honey, the pohlice have got your name and your number. (*Sees* JUDY.) Who is this?

KATY. Judy. Vick's roommate.

JUEL LAURIE. What happened to him?

KATY (*looking at the* MUSCLE MAN, *who is watching her*). I killed him.

JUEL LAURIE. What did you do that for?

KATY. I just did.

JUEL LAURIE. He got a knife hole on his rib. Vick, get up from him like that.

KATY. Leave him alone, Juel Laurie.

JUEL LAURIE. Now the pohlice will drag you off for sure.

KATY. They would have anyway. And I'm too tired to care.

JUEL LAURIE (*looking suddenly surprised, turning to the* MUSCLE MAN). He was on this man, won't he?

KATY. What do you mean?

JUEL LAURIE. He was on this man. That's what it was. Don't shake your head at me, I know. (*Moves closer to the* MUSCLE MAN.) You should be ashamed of yourself.

> (VICK *stands, looks at the bandages, then drops the bandages and gets the dress.*)

VICK (*to* KATY). Here's your dress.

> (VICK *helps* KATY *put on the dress.*)

VICK. They'll be up here in a minute.

KATY. I know.

VICK. They did say somebody called. (*Looks at* JUDY.) I wonder who it was.

KATY. It don't matter now.

VICK. Poor baby. He didn't have anybody. Anybody at all.

KATY. He had you.

JUEL LAURIE. There's a dead boy on the floor.

VICK. There sure is, honey. (*To* KATY.) I brought you a pair of pumps too. It was hard to find the right pair in the dark.

KATY. How do I look?

VICK. You need to fix your hair. Juel Laurie, run to my bathroom and find me a brush or a comb.

JUEL LAURIE. Vanice says the pohlice could be here any second.

VICK. I know, and Katy's not quite ready yet. Find me a brush like I asked you to. She's got a long night ahead of her and I want her to look just right.

(*Exit* JUEL LAURIE.)

KATY. Will you call my mama? Tell her I'll talk to her when I can? (*Almost breaks down.*) Tell her I ain't no bad girl, please tell her.

VICK. I'll tell her.

(*Enter* JUEL LAURIE, *with hairbrush.*)

JUEL LAURIE. It was on the back of the toilet with a hair net on it.

VICK (*brushing* KATY's *hair*). Thank you ma'am. Do you hear anything?

JUEL LAURIE (*going to the door*). Vanice says no. They're still right down there shooting the shit, right where the landlord bordered up the window.

(*The* MUSCLE MAN *comes closer to them, then stops.*)

JUEL LAURIE. You got blood on you.

VICK. He can't help it, Juel Laurie.

KATY. You need to take care of him.

VICK. I will in a minute.

KATY. No. I mean you need to take care of him from now on.

VICK. He'll be gone as soon as I find out who he is.

KATY. He ain't nobody. He just walking around in the world. I know him from the minute I saw him. You want to stay here with Vick, don't you big man? You want to stay right here and let Vick take good care of you.

VICK. Hush, Katy.

JUEL LAURIE. The pohlice got their hands on their guns. They say they answering a call. They pulling down their belts like the cowboys.

KATY. I know what I'm talking about. You're going to stay right here, ain't that right? Ain't that what you came for?

VICK. He can't understand you.

KATY. He can understand me just fine.

VICK. You got such nice hair.

KATY. I feel good now. I feel real good. I feel like I'm sitting out on the levee watching the river.

VICK. I thought I heard a ship horn a little while ago.

KATY. You know it didn't even feel like I was doing anything to that man in the motel.

VICK. Hush.

KATY. Will they make me meet his wife?

VICK. I don't think so.

KATY. She look so sweet in her picture.

JUEL LAURIE. They on the stairs now, coming up.

VICK. It's all right. Katy's almost ready.

KATY. Go see my baby girl. You'll do that for me, won't you? And tell stories about her mama.

VICK. Yes baby, I will.

KATY. I love my baby girl. I really do.

VICK. I know.

JUEL LAURIE. They knocking on my door now, but I'm not there, and Vanice don't let nobody in when he's alone. They're knocking but he don't care. (*Laughs, as if she sees it.*) That's right. Turn away. Nobody home.

VICK. They'll tear this place to pieces.

KATY. Yes ma'am, they will.

(*Voices and footsteps outside.*)

VICK. I wonder where I put this man's clothes. I guess I'll have to dress him and bring him down to the station.

KATY. They're in the bathroom.

VICK. I better go see.

(*Exit* VICK.

KATY *crosses to face the* MUSCLE MAN.)

JUEL LAURIE. You look good Katy Jume. The pohlice going to want to eat you up.

KATY (*to the* MUSCLE MAN). You owe me for this, motherfucker.

JUEL LAURIE. I had me a fine red dress like that one time. From Maison Blanche.

(*Knock on the door.*)

But I couldn't find no clutch that would go. Worried me to death.

(*Knock on the door.*)

Somebody ought to open that. The pohlice is here.

KATY. I will. Even though this is not my home.

(*Lights fade as she goes to the door.*

Light lingers on the MUSCLE MAN, *who kneels at* JUDY'S
  side.
*He touches the wound and smears the red on himself, as
  before.*
When VICK *enters, the* MUSCLE MAN *stands and faces*
  VICK.
Lights continue to fade as VICK *sets down the clothes.*)

VICK. You've got blood on you again. What am I going to do with
  you?

  (*Street noise rises.*
  VICK *and the* MUSCLE MAN *face each other as lights fade
    to black.*
  Last of all, the sound of the SAXOPHONE PLAYER *blowing
    Judy's theme from the street outside.*)

Reynolds Price, on *The Lizard of Tarsus*

iven the fact that religious emotions—adoration, dread, praise, and supplication—lie at the origins of drama throughout the world, it's odd to note that the life of Jesus has played so small a role on the Western stage. With the exception of a few medieval mystery plays and the occasional modern Passion play or Christmas pageant, there has been no supremely successful and enduring theatrical work concerned with any portion of his endlessly engaging life. And the causes of that absence are interesting to consider.

For centuries after the Middle Ages, many Western societies simply forbade the portrayal of Christ and his companions on stage. Shakespeare, for instance, could not legally have presented a play on the subject; nor could virtually any other sizable later playwright in Europe or America. Churches and governments had decreed that the riveting drama of so many episodes in Jesus' life —primarily the matchless conflict and triumph of his final week —would be confined to readings from the gospel accounts and symbolic commemorations of his sacrifices in the visible rites of the Mass and in ecclesiastical music.

And when those public bans began to expire in the twentieth century, no single figure stepped forward to reclaim the lost subject. Thus Bach remains the sole Western genius to have provided, in his Passions, a Jesus drama that endures among us, however unsuited for theatrical production. It remains to be seen if any of the numerous, and intermittently impressive, Jesus films of recent history will achieve such longevity. (I suspect that long stretches of Scorsese's *The Last Temptation of Christ* will prove compelling in their freshness and visual precision.)

Why are there no contenders from those artists whose predilections would seem to have compelled them toward direct theatrical engagement with the story—Samuel Beckett, say, or Ingmar Bergman or Horton Foote; why nothing from Stravinsky, a devout Orthodox Christian, to stand beside his still-vital *Oedipus Rex*? If I had to venture a single guess at an explanation, I'd suggest that the patently historical drama as relayed to us by the oldest gospel (Mark) and the eyewitness gospel (John) has effectively blanked the field. The access to narrative magnetism and the dramatic power of those two writers have proved so nearly inimitable as to discourage competition from extraordinary writers.

Yet here is Jim Grimsley engaging the tale in one of its later aspects—an aspect that's implicit but unacknowledged in the New Testament. In his first three novels and some of his earlier plays, Grimsley's clarity of gaze at the poles of human evil and victory in ongoing Christian (like it or not) culture goes far toward validating his daring in *The Lizard of Tarsus*. What living American or English novelist has more unquestionably *earned* his credentials? Yet even Grimsley balks at a direct examination of the traditional story within its own framework of time and place.

He sets his invented action at an unspecified moment in a vaguely present world, a time shortly after the promised Second Coming of Jesus—or J., as this figure, with some degree of deference, is called. And the language, props, and costumes suggest our own era. Those cautionary gestures aside, Grimsley proceeds with a blistering intensity of welcome quality of humor (some of it broad) to embody before us one of the central confrontations that continue to invigorate and torment the weakened but still-presiding faith of our civilization—the endless debate between Rabbi Jesus of Nazareth, a provincial healer and teacher who ran afoul of the religious establishment of his own people and their Roman overlords, and Paul of Tarsus, whom Jesus never knew but who is almost single-handedly responsible for the astonishingly rapid spread of a cult about Jesus throughout the world.

Writers as recent and powerful as Nietzsche and Shaw have probed, in essays, the implications of that confrontation; but no writer known to me has poised that battle on an actual stage and turned it so many ways to the light. I'd give a good deal to see and hear *The Lizard of Tarsus* in a vivid production by a brave director of ferocious taste and with the three great actors required by Grimsley's arctic words and burning strength of judgment and mercy. I suspect I'd come away eager to see the play again, to read it more slowly from time to time, and to tend the still-raw flesh that haunts most believers who face the indispensable yet perpetually baleful mind and voice of that immense thinker, lover, and hater —Paul (born Saul in the city of Tarsus), who molds our lives still.

THE LIZARD OF TARSUS

The Lizard of Tarsus premiered at Seven Stages Theatre in Atlanta in January 1990, in a production directed by the author, featuring Jim Peck as J., Del Hamilton as Paul, and Faye Allen as Sol Heiffer. The set was designed by Roy McGhee. Sound design was by Brian Engel.

The play was subsequently produced in New York at the Triangle Theatre Company by Harland Productions and the Triangle Theatre Company, directed by Joseph Megel, with John Pietrowski as J. Jim Ligon as Paul, and Elisabeth Lewis Corley as Sol Heiffer. E. David Cosier designed the set; Christopher Gorzelnick, the lights; and Dean Gray, the sound.

J., a political prisoner

PAUL, an inquisitor; male, serpentine, good looking, oily, politically shrewd. Age can vary.

SOL HEIFFER, a follower of Paul; a woman of uncommon appearance

SETTING

A bleak room like a prison cell—stone walls, stark lighting, a bench with a thin mattress, very uncomfortable looking. Rough furniture. A crucifix on the wall, the figure grotesque but only partly visible.

Lights rise on J., *lying on the mattress, arms over his face.*
Enter PAUL, *with a large file and several pencils.*

PAUL. Are you ready to continue our discussion?

J. Is that what you call what we're doing?

PAUL. Wouldn't you?

J. No, I don't think so.

PAUL. But aren't we like two friends having a long talk? Aren't we getting close like that, the longer we talk?

J. Do you feel close to me?

PAUL. Yes, I do. I feel as if I'm standing inside your skin. I feel as if I'm thinking your thoughts along with you. Do you mind? Do you feel close to me?

J. Yes.

PAUL. Have you been worshiping? While I was away?

J. Yes.

PAUL. How? What were you doing?

J. I was listening.

PAUL. What were you listening to?

J. I was listening, I was, just listening.

PAUL. What did you hear?

> (J. *rises from the bed, paces back and forth in long,*
> *somnambulant strides, hesitates.*)

J. What were the sounds from outside? The people.

PAUL. When? Just now?

J. Yes. (*Pause.*) I can still hear it.

PAUL. There's a crowd. You aren't surprised, are you? There's always a crowd when you show up. (*Pause.*) Careful not to walk too much. You've been asleep. Quite a while.

J. Was I drugged?

PAUL. Sedated. You were sedated. After we talked.

J. Was I?

PAUL. Mildly.

J. How long are you going to keep me here?

PAUL. There's nothing wrong with the room, is there? It's a pleasant room. Really. There's a good breeze through here. Stand under the window, you can smell the market. You can smell it, can't you? The meat cooking and the candy turning in the stainless steel pots, and the beer.

J. I don't smell any of that.

PAUL. It's really a very nice room. You'll agree with me, given a little time. The colors are very warm, in sunlight. It's never very cold. It's never too warm. I think it's perfect for you. You'll be very happy here. You'll rest. Your mind will find its perfect resonance. These stones are like harmony.

J. I don't hear the stones.

PAUL. Who does?

J. You were talking about harmony. From them.

PAUL. The harmony is in their perfect silence. (*Pause.*) You seem surprised that I said that. Do you think I have no sensitivity for such things? Do you think I cannot listen as you do, to a music that is beyond music?

J. Do you hear music?

PAUL. Hear what?

J. Nothing. Never mind.

PAUL. Of course. Music. I hear it clearly, with my whole being. The great cosmic throbbing. (*Pause.*) What did you tell the people in the market?

J. I tried not to tell them anything, I only wanted to buy an orange.

PAUL. You appeared without any warning apart from all your followers and spoke from Blind John's News and Magazine Emporium; the whole crowd was talking about it. You knew we would learn of your appearance, but you spoke anyway. And now your followers are making music and smashing their stereo components in the streets.

J. I only wanted to buy an orange and there was a boy with a Walkman in my way.

PAUL. The Word is spreading but nobody will tell us what it is.

J. What word?

PAUL. You told them there is a higher music. We know that much.

J. I might have told them that.

PAUL. And everyone threw radios in the streets. Little red and green wires everywhere.

J. I was short of breath. The pollen in Jerusalem this time of year. I had forgotten.

PAUL. You told them there is a hiss behind every other sound. Older than every other sound. The voice of eternity. They were all talking about it. (*Pause.*) I've heard that sound more times than I can remember. In fact, I very often contemplate the sound from the beginning of time. Isn't it strange that we should be so much alike? As if our minds had been working in harmony all this time.

(*Silence.*)

PAUL. What did you tell the people in the market?

J. I can hear the lizard climbing up the wall outside. Breathless. Can you hear it? Him?

PAUL. Yes, I can. In fact I saw it—saw him—when I was returning from the Arcade, just now. A beautiful reptile, covered with horns and gray skin, sunning itself on a rock, in perfect agreement with its surroundings. His surroundings. We were aware of each other, the lizard and I.

J. He needs the shade this time of day.

PAUL. Of course, you're right. I must have seen him earlier.

J. He sits in the sun in the morning. After dawn. It's hard to move that early. He's cold, stiff. He's hungry. There's not much time. He finds the first patch of sun and drinks it, his blood stirs and he becomes awake. In the morning.

(*Silence.*)

PAUL. Welcome back, by the way.

J. Thank you.

PAUL. Is this second visit very different from the first?

J. The city is very much the same.

PAUL. I don't know why that surprises me. (*Pause.*) We've waited a very long time.

J. Really?

PAUL. Ages.

J. Well, you've kept yourself up.

PAUL (*after a moment*). You do move in mysterious ways, don't

you. That's why your return has taken us by surprise. Even
though we expected it. (*Laughs.*) I know I've done all I could
do to be prepared. Founding missions, writing letters, that sort
of thing. But I expect you know that.

J. No, I hadn't heard.

(*Silence.*)

PAUL. Did I tell you it is better not to marry?

J. No, you didn't.

PAUL. Are you married?

J. No.

PAUL. It is better not to. It is better to be as I am. Chaste. Those
who cannot be chaste should marry, of course, in recognition
of their own weakness. But it is better not to.

J. Could I have something to eat?

PAUL. I have a letter about it. I could show it to you.

J. I'm very hungry.

PAUL. Man does not live by bread alone. (*Pause.*) I could have married, of course. If I had wanted to. In Tarsus, I was considered
very good looking.

J. (*as if to himself*). I wanted an orange. We had been walking all
day, my followers and I. Through the crowds. They kept recog-
nizing me and asking for my autograph. (*Laughs softly.*) I've
had so many names, I almost forgot which one to use.

PAUL. Remind me later, we need to get a list of your aliases.

J. (*still to himself*). I've been thrown to the dogs in so many places.
Every two-bit world you can think of. Wherever two or more
of you are gathered. That's a laugh.

PAUL. I'd like to talk to you about that. I feel as if I may have had
similar experiences of martyrdom.

J. Could I have a cigarette?

PAUL. I didn't know you smoked. (*Pause.*) No. I don't have any.

J. Send for one. Send for an orange.

PAUL. Which do you want? The orange? Or the cigarette?

J. (*lying on the cot again, turning away from him*). You won't bring either one.

PAUL (*opening the file*). Do you want to know what happened to all your friends?

J. What friends?

PAUL. Your followers. From the last time. I have a lot of the information right here. Do you want to hear it? (*No response.*) For instance, your mother. She certainly did well for herself over the ages.

J. Please stop.

PAUL. Shrines in every major city, prayer chapels doing a booming business, her face appearing on the sides of water tanks and in obscure Mexican huts. Miracles in lush garden spots. Quite an end for a little girl from the wrong side of Bethlehem.

J. She had a gift for simple living.

PAUL. Oh, that's very droll. Yes. Yes, apparently she did. Not everyone had it so nice. (*Lifts a piece of paper, shakes head.*) Lots of crosses. Tortures. That kind of thing. But this. Poor John.

J. John?

PAUL. Remember? The one who always had his head on your bosom?

> (*A crowd is heard for the first time, restless, murmuring,
> like a hive of insects.*
> PAUL *lays down the file.*)

PAUL. So now they know which building. Perhaps even which window.

J. My mother lives in Orange County. California.

PAUL. What did you say?

J. You were asking about my mother. She's given up charitable works at the present. She writes greeting cards.

PAUL. I hope you find this amusing.

J. I'm serious. You did want information, didn't you?

PAUL. What do you tell people when I'm not listening? What do you say? (*Pause; no answer.*) I had a woman follow you. With a cassette recorder and three blank tapes. And then you gave your message and the people around her took the cassette recorder and smashed it against a fire hydrant. And they wound the tapes around her and stuffed them in her mouth. And the mob destroyed a camcorder as well. I don't know who sent that, I hadn't thought of video. (*Pause.*) You should write your teachings down.

J. That's never a good idea.

PAUL. But if you don't write them down, someone will write them down for you. And they always get it wrong, afterward. (*Listens to the crowd sound, which has continued all this while, in varying degrees.*) Listen to them. Do you think they want to save you this time? Or kill you? Or what?

J. I suppose that all depends on you, doesn't it?

　　　　(*Silence.*)

PAUL. Did I tell you what happened, to me, after you died? Not the whole story. Just the part about the road to Damascus.

J. Something wonderful, I suppose.

PAUL (*laughing*). But you must know. You were there.

J. Was I? I can't remember.

PAUL. We had just arranged the stoning of Stephen Wiggins. At the old Arcade, not the new one. You remember Stephen, don't you? We stoned him, for cause. For professing belief in you, of a religious nature. We drew a great crowd. I could tell some of the people there had heard you talk before you died. So I asked them to tell me what you had said. Just that. But they couldn't. Even the ones who tried. And finally Stephen Wiggins told me, "You will never understand, Saul. Never." So we stoned him, because he could not explain what he meant.

J. Stephen was a very nice man.

PAUL. His wife was a lovely woman. Do you remember her? Ruth Henderson Wiggins. Henderson being her maiden name, of course.

J. She was always very kind to me.

PAUL. What always puzzled me about Wiggins. I never for a moment felt he meant any harm. By what he told me. (*Laughs.*) He was right. As it turns out. He had a way. (*Pause.*) Anyway, there was a lovely funeral and I went, of course. Everyone went. And then I took a weekend trip somewhere. Damascus. I knew a girl. In those days everybody knew a girl in Damascus. Packed my bags and took off, just enough for the weekend. Well, about halfway there, as I was riding along in the desert, I saw this light. This blinding bright light. (*To* J.) Does any of this sound familiar?

J. Yes. Somewhat familiar.

PAUL. I pulled over. I took out my Polaroid but got no picture. Just this kind of cloudy void. Then a voice issued out of the light, and you asked me that famous question. "Saul, Saul, why persecutest thou me?" You remember?

J. Something like that.

PAUL. Then I told you, it's because when you were alive and walking around with all your followers, I felt alienated from you. I felt a despair and a worthlessness which soon changed to bitter hatred within my soul. Whenever I was around you and your followers, you would never say anything. To other people you said wise things, and you did miracles. But when I was around you never did anything except look at me like I was some kind of creep. The only thing I ever got to see you do was throw the vending machines out of the Temple. And you answered, with this voice out of this blinding light, that you were sorry and that you would now tell me what you had been teaching everybody, right there. Then you did. Then you struck me blind.

(*Silence in the room.*

The crowd continues to murmur outside.)

J. Was anybody with you when all this happened?

PAUL. No, of course not. I was alone. As you were alone in your own days of desert temptation. Splendid isolation. Merciless sun beating down. The whole desolation scenario. Later there were others involved: Sam Jennings and Bert Bryant, who found me standing next to the car, blind, tears streaming down my face. Singing along with the car radio. Me. I had never sung in public before in my life.

J. How did you know I was talking to you?

PAUL. You called my name. You did.

(J. *scratches his head as if he cannot remember.*)

PAUL. There wasn't anybody else there for you to talk to.

J. So Sam and Bert took care of you.

PAUL. They took me to a Days Inn in Damascus. Bert drove my car. (*Pause.*) If I asked you. Would you consider giving a deposition? About the events of that day, just as I have described them?

J. You mean, formally.

PAUL. Yes. (*Pause.*) There have been certain challenges. To my authority. Of late. (*Pause.*) My attorneys will arrange the whole process. If you agree.

J. I'm not sure how much I can remember.

PAUL. But I just told you the whole story. Just repeat that.

J. But won't they want my point of view?

>(*Enter* SOL HEIFFER, *dragging a large Bible on a chain that is fastened around her waist, like a belt.*
>
>*She hands a file to* PAUL.
>
>*Exit* SOL HEIFFER. *She should move with some difficulty.*
>
>PAUL *scans the file.*
>
>*He is disturbed by what he reads, closes the file.*)

PAUL. Remove your outer garment.

J. Pardon?

PAUL. Take off your shirt.

>(J. *removes outer garment.*
>
>*Beneath,* J. *wears a thin shirt, the back of which is blood soaked.*)

J. This is very uncivilized.

PAUL. Please. Do as I ask.

>(J. *removes shirt, facing audience.*
>
>PAUL *inspects* J.*'s back, grimacing at the sight.*)

PAUL. Who did this?

J. My followers.

>(*Suddenly the crowd noise swells.*)

PAUL. Someone is passing out leaflets. In the market and at the New Arcade. Pictures of you. Of this. (*Gestures to* J.*'s back.*) Listen to that mob. You're responsible for this. You. Inflammatory. Barbaric. (PAUL *holds up one of the flyers and shakes it.*) Filth. Inflammatory filth. As if we would have you beaten. When we've waited all these years. Seven bridesmaids with our lamps full.

J. They were able to afford color.

PAUL. What?

J. We had wanted to use color. On the flyer. But we were low on budget.

>(*Enter* SOL HEIFFER, *with a tray of first-aid supplies.*
>
>PAUL *takes the tray; exit* SOL HEIFFER.)

PAUL. Sit down.

>(J. *sits.*
>
>PAUL *sits behind* J. *on the narrow bed and begins to wash his back.*
>
>*After a moment, in perfect silence, he produces an orange from his robe and hands it to* J.)

J. Thank you.

>(J. *peels the orange slowly.*)

PAUL. Of course you felt no pain. When you were beaten.

J. None. (*Pause.*) Or rather, I felt a great deal.

PAUL (*laughing softly, as if in perfect understanding*). Both at once. I understand perfectly.

J. Are you angry?

PAUL. Only that you would cause this yourself. That you would allow this to happen to you. (*Is overcome by empathy.*) So much depends on you. On your well-being. And you're so careless of your health.

J. One cannot think of such things.

PAUL. Of course not. But still. (*Reaches sensitive fingertips toward the wounds, withdraws before touch is completed.*) Still. Such things. As these raw wounds on your poor back. Such transcendent suffering. (*Pause.*) Like my poor servant. The wretched creature who brought this tray into the room. What a miserable story. Lost her tongue in a horrible. Horrible. (*Pause.*) But I was telling you about John.

J. Were you?

PAUL. I'm sure he would like to see you.

J. Is he still in town?

PAUL. Yes. Very close by.

J. Do you really think I might see him? Or are you playing a game?

PAUL. I'd be very glad for you to see him. Very glad to arrange it. (*Pause.*) He's not the same man, these days.

J. He would be a good deal older.

PAUL. He was crazy without you.

J. We were very close.

> (PAUL *rises slowly behind* J., *looking down at his back.*
> *He speaks as he rises.*)

PAUL. One could see that you were. (*Pause.*) He held himself together pretty well, without you. I only knew him after you were gone, of course. In his decline. But even then. Such a dreamy man. Eyes to drown in. (*Pause.*) He spoke of himself as the one whom you loved. I often wondered what he meant by that. (*Pause.*) I tried not to resent him, of course. I only saw you together once. You and John. At the Arcade, the old one. You were drinking a root beer, and John had a cherry cola. You were impeccable. He had flaked ice on his chin, a thin red line running down his neck. The way he watched you. I'll never forget it. One wouldn't have thought either of you was about to die for the sins of the world.

J. You say he's not himself.

PAUL. Oh no. Hasn't been for some time. Ever since he finished that last book, I forget the title. He's in West End Mental Health Center.

> (J. *is visibly disturbed for the first time.*
> *He moves restlessly in the cell.*)

PAUL. He has good days. Perfectly lucid. You wouldn't know what he'd been through, the shipwreck, the days on the island, the Four Horsemen, the visions. He can't control them, poor fellow. You're sitting there having a nice cup of coffee with him and the next thing you know he's off in the belly of the Beast. (*Pause;* PAUL *lifts* J.'s *bloody shirt from wherever it has fallen.*) I always thought it was the strain of losing you.

> (*Enter* SOL HEIFFER, *with a clean shirt.*
> *She hands the clean shirt to* PAUL, *takes the bloody one;*
> *exit* SOL HEIFFER.
> PAUL *helps* J. *with the shirt.*)

PAUL. What did you tell the people in the market?

J. Did I thank you for the orange?

PAUL. Yes.

J. Do you have a cigarette?

PAUL. I have asthma. I would prefer that you don't smoke.

> (*Silence.*)

PAUL. You should understand by now. It's mine anyway. The message. If you don't give me the Word, I'll get it somewhere. Someone will tell.

J. Do you hear music? Now?

PAUL (*listening*). No. Nothing I can make out above the crowd.

J. Listen again. (*Listens.*) It's him. In the shade. The lizard.

PAUL. I don't hear anything.

J. He's so hot he's humming. Drowsing. Dreaming of flies.

PAUL. You can't possibly hear anything so faint. Through these walls.

J. I don't need to hear him. I know he's there. Waiting patiently.

PAUL. I wonder if I will ever be so sublime. (*Pause.*) Why don't you teach the mob to sing, if you want music.

> (*Silence.*)

J. Tell me what you have planned.

PAUL. For what? For you?

J. Yes.

PAUL. Well of course that's all very complicated. We will go through several stages of you. I'm afraid I can't share many of the details. (*Pause.*) But we will allow you to plead your cause sufficiently. Justice to be served and all that. We are well aware of your position.

J. So you will let me out of here soon.

PAUL. Well I didn't say that. Exactly. Your present detention is a matter of policy and I, of course, am merely one voice. Among equal apostolic voices.

J. You said you would let me speak.

PAUL. I believe I used the phrase "plead your cause sufficiently." We are suggesting that you make some use of pamphlets and other religious tracts of the sort that we always have to invent later anyway. We thought perhaps you could compose them from here.

J. From my cell.

PAUL. I think it's a very romantic image. The preacher from the wild, fresh from his triumphant Second Coming, writing from the fiery depths of his soul. Imprisoned but bravely carrying on with his ministry. In the last moments of his. Well. You see, I almost gave it away. (*Pause.*) That's a later stage, of course.

J. What is?

PAUL. These are the last days of your life. Naturally.

J. This is too early. You know it perfectly well. I haven't done everything I'm supposed to do. (*No response.*) You should set me free. A few more days at least.

PAUL. I'm afraid you've spoilt any chance of that. With your jaunt

into the market to buy an orange. You've upset a lot of people
with that. A lot of my colleagues.

J. You know I don't upset people deliberately. My end of this is not
very pleasant, either.

PAUL. Oh don't look at me. I'm perfectly happy with the whole
arrangement.

(*Silence.*)

J. I can't make do with pamphlets and tracts. I'm sorry.

PAUL. You're really not in any position to be stubborn.

J. There's no life in pamphlets. Writing down a parable isn't the
same thing as telling it.

PAUL. But what you lose in immediacy you gain in convenience.
Look at the beauty of it. From our perspective. I'm just asking
you to listen with an open mind. You write the pamphlets, sign
them, we do a little picture. Maybe you sitting on the bed
looking haggard and divine, something like that. Light from
the window, this beam, we can rig something. I'll call Aaron.
You do a few tracts. You write down some of your favorite say-
ings, the really great cryptic stuff. Then, when you're—when
this whole thing is over with—we don't have the usual documentation crisis. Everything you want remembered is right
down there on paper, black and white, crystal clear. See?

J. You'll let me write anything I like.

PAUL. Of course. I'll edit. Nothing major. A few doctrinal correc-
tions here and there.

(*Enter* SOL HEIFFER, *with a small electronic typewriter
or a computer on a rolling cart.*)

J. You'd like to begin this at once, I see.

PAUL. Well we might give it a start. (*To* SOL HEIFFER.) Do you have
a report for me?

> (SOL HEIFFER *produces a crumpled parchment with per-*
> *forations, indicating it was computer generated.*
> PAUL *lets her bring it to him and reads it.*)

PAUL. Food fights in your name in major restaurants all over the city. Chaos spreading to the malls in the outlying areas of Palestine. The police are helpless. Your closest disciples have gone into hiding. The major television stations are doing live reports and preparing special analyses. Your photograph as we dragged you from the New Arcade will be on the cover of every weekly newsmagazine, as well as periodicals devoted to various types of personality cults. (*Pause.*) Your first pamphlet, once you compose it, will simply help the massive wave of publicity to crest and wash us all to sea. Your triumph. Complete.

J. I can't write.

PAUL. You mean, I suppose, that you consider yourself to be morally and ethically incapable of writing.

J. I can't read either.

PAUL (*after silence*). I see I am to be frustrated in all my choices. Well, perhaps we can obtain dictating equipment for you.

J. (*to* SOL HEIFFER). Come here.

> (SOL HEIFFER *checks with* PAUL, *who agrees that she can*
> *do as asked.*
> SOL HEIFFER *approaches* J.
> *He touches her jaw, frames it with his open hand.*)

J. I am sorry for what happened to you.

> (*She embraces him slowly, gradually realizing he is not*
> *making fun of her.*)

J. (*to* PAUL). She likes you, I think.

PAUL. Does she? How nice.

J. She's very devoted to you. She thinks you're a good man.

PAUL. I'm certain I'm all the better for her good opinion.

J. I'd be glad about it, if I were you.

PAUL (*dismissing* SOL HEIFFER *with a gesture*). I am glad. I am always glad for the faith of simple people. Their simple love magnifies me. Immensely. Do you think my connection with Sol is any less deep or instinctive than yours?

J. Perhaps you could simply write down what I tell you.

PAUL. I beg your pardon.

J. To get your pamphlets done.

PAUL. We were discussing the peasant class. The poor. Which ye shall have with ye always, to coin a phrase.

J. There's some doubt as to whether I ever actually said that.

PAUL. There you have it. The value of documentation in a nutshell. (*Pause.*) Sol is already looking for a Dictaphone. She's very efficient. As for the transcription, Jerusalem is full of young transcriptionists this time of year. (*Pause.*) Have I told you the horrible story of the poor woman's tongue? Ripped out by ravening tax collectors when she professed that a love of Christ had led her to vow poverty, and that she had no money for taxes. Since tax collectors have to collect something, they took her tongue. She was left for dead in an alley behind a stock brokerage. I found her and with my prayers moved the face of heaven to restore her to health. No one could restore her tongue, poor thing. We sued, of course. Her case was very famous, defended by F. Lee Bailey. The settlement was generous, and of course Sol Heiffer donated all of it to our work. She has devoted her life to good works here in the chambers of the Inquisitentiary. (*Pause.*) She would be embarrassed if she knew I had told you her story. Since her sufferings are so paltry, compared to yours.

> (J. *produces a cigarette from his flowing garment and*
> *lights it.*)

PAUL. Do you have another?

J. No. Sorry.

PAUL. That's quite all right.

> (PAUL *produces a cigarette from his own robe and*
> *lights it.*
> *They smoke for a few moments in silence.*
> *Then* J. *grinds the cigarette carefully out, putting the*
> *butt back into his flowing garment.*)

PAUL (*continuing to smoke*). Frugal. Do your followers know about this nasty habit?

J. Some. We used to smoke cigarettes in the desert.

PAUL. Forty days and forty nights, what could you do? (*Pause.*) I often think my own desert journey was akin to yours. My blindness. The awful terror of your voice. The cold fear in my heart. After all, why was I persecuting you? What could the answer be? (*Laughs in gentle revelation.*) I suppose Satan was also behind me. Whispering in my ear. Showing me great towers and kingdoms. Do you suppose?

J. I'm sure the two events were very similar.

PAUL. I knew, I understood at once. Even before you spoke to me out of that blinding cloud. The message was already there, in my heart. Or so I thought. For a long time. Traveling through the whole world, telling people about you, about what I thought you meant, about the whole picture, love, faith, healing, the power of forgiveness, the need for good works. Everything. Then you returned and you went shopping for an orange in the market and you spoke to the people impromptu, standing on a melon cart, and what you said is anybody's

guess. And now, chaos everywhere. Riot in the streets. People
are drinking beer and dancing with their clothes loose. Breaking windshields and stringing fiber-optic cable in the trees.
Killing mosquitoes with their bare hands in the night. Such
things had been outlawed, and now chaos has returned. You
decreed this by proclamation extempore from the top of a
fruit cart in downtown Jerusalem. (*Pause.*) This is not what we
wanted, not what we expected. This is not the glorious silver
station wagon sailing down on a cloud of radiance from the
east. This is not one thousand years of peaceful shopping in
the mall. So I wonder who you really are and what you really
wanted that day in the desert.

J. I've told you, it's hard for me to remember.

PAUL. Try.

J. I'm sorry.

> (*Silence.*)

PAUL. You have no idea how important this is to me.

J. It was a long time ago. What difference can it make, what I remember or what I don't remember?

PAUL. Challenges. Oh I know you don't think much of this sort of
thing. But there are certain challenges. Dogmatic and otherwise. To my current authority. And I have rested much of my
authority on the miracle of my conversion. Along with impeccable scholarship, worldwide vision and a letter-writing talent
second to none. The David O. Selznick of religion. But I have
my enemies. I know you have little sympathy. But it would be
such a help if you could substantiate my story. Lay claim to
some of my works. Paul, my good and faithful servant, that
kind of thing. You have no idea how valuable such a reference
would be. In certain circles.

J. I had no idea your circumstances were so difficult.

PAUL. Part of it's your fault. You've taken your sweet time with this return trip.

J. One makes no promises where one's timetable is concerned. I go to prepare a mansion for you. Remember? Mansions take time.

PAUL. Well that's very nice. I know what you mean. You think you leave me behind when you get cryptic like that, but I follow you. But I have some news for you. Mansions or not, we nearly lost this one. You and me. We nearly lost this place. Listen to that mob. (*They listen.*) Another couple of centuries and even you couldn't have quieted them. Listen to that howling. Listen.

J. Plowshares.

PAUL. Pardon?

J. Plowshares. Into swords. Remember? (*Pause.*) Oh. You weren't there for that.

PAUL. I read about it.

J. It isn't the same.

PAUL. Why not? Tell me. Tell me what you said, tell me a parable.

J. It's no use, Paul.

PAUL. Why not?

J. I can't remember. And even if I could. A parable is born out of its peculiar fold of space and time, specific to a particular moment-place complex. A parable is for wherever you are, your personal space. You can't just recite it. Anywhere you like.

PAUL. Tell me a parable. For this moment.

J. I wish it were that simple.

PAUL. But it is. For you. It is.

J. (*thoughtfully*). I shouldn't even consider this.

PAUL. I'm begging you. Just once. Just once, tell me something.

J. You're not recording this.

PAUL. No. I swear.

J. You promise not to write this down.

PAUL. I promise.

J. Not even afterward. When all this stuff is finished. (*Pause.*) Because I'd like to tell you one of the parables from the B list. We usually stick to the A list.

PAUL. I swear. I'll never write this down. Never.

J. (*thinking of a parable*). Well. (*Still thinking.*) Well, in a certain country there lived a man with sons by three different wives, and the youngest of these sons was very fair, and his name was Emur. And the father loved Emur more than he loved his other sons, even though by rights he should have shown favor to his eldest son, Nathan. He also had thirteen daughters but they don't figure into this parable. Well, Nathan became jealous of his youngest brother, Emur, and one day when they were hunting, Nathan led Emur astray down a sidewise path, away from the hunting party that his father was leading. And this was a woeful and a dark path down which Nathan led Emur. And because it was hot, Emur removed his outer garments and revealed his splendid young muscular body, tawny gold colored and rippling with strength. Nathan was wroth with rage at the sight of his near-naked brother, and his lips trembled, and his blood boiled, and he saith to himself, "Woe will be done here on this sidewise path where I have lured my youngest brother, for verily I say, he is a pretty boy." And Nathan fell on Emur and had his way with him and afterward slew him, for he could not bear to have his brother look at him. Even though they had just enjoyed themselves very much. And Nathan looked down at the body of his slain dead brother whom he had killed, and Nathan cried out in horror and said, "O Lord, I have murdered my brother which did love me truly." And he ran to his father where his father was hunting, and he fell down at his father's feet and clung to them and said, "O Father, I have slain my brother Emur." And the father said, "Why son have you slain your brother Emur?" And Nathan answered, "Because when my member was in his mouth I became racked with guilt and did repent having lured him down that sidewise path." And the father raised up Nathan and said, "That's okay my son. You didn't mean any harm. And because you are my flesh I forgive you." Then they buried Emur amid great feasting and weeping which was attended by many tribes and peoples. And among these peoples was the fair Naomi. The fair Naomi came to Nathan in the garden beyond the market gate, being a poor daughter of a distant male relative, but very fair, and Nathan knew not Naomi, but Naomi knew Nathan. And Nathan took one look at the fair Naomi and his eyes popped out. And soon they were married. Then a great plague came and wiped out the whole grape crop for seven years, and Nathan one day looked at Naomi, who was barren also, and said, "Accursed are you among women, for you were fair to me when I first saw you, but now you are as a seedless seed and a grapeless grape, and I despise you and I spit on you. For you have brought bad crops to my father." And Nathan slew Naomi in a great rage. And then he looked at her pitiful body in the dust and said, "Woe. Woe." And he fled to his father where his father was hunting and he clung to the feet of his father and said, "O Father, pity me and spare me from iniquity, for I have just slain my wife, Naomi, who was barren." And the father raised him up and said, "That's okay my son.

For you are a basically good boy with a sudden temper, and you have to expect this kind of thing." And Nathan was waxed happy and said joyfully, "My father is a good guy and knoweth all things well."

PAUL. This is very interesting.

J. There's more. In his twenty-fifth year Nathan had a son, Norris, by his concubine Edna. And Edna was a beefy, chunky woman whom Nathan feared somewhat, so that after a time he chained her in the basement. For she wished him to make her his wife and he was content that she should remain his concubine as before. So therefore Nathan raised Norris without any knowledge that his mother was chained steadfastly in the basement. And Norris grew fair and fat, eating many doughnuts and cookies. Till one day God appeared to Norris in the form of a jelly glazed and said unto Norris, "Norris. Your mother languishes in the basement bound steadfastly and still you do nothing. Wherefore have you forsaken your mother who bore you in her womb?" And Norris reached for the jelly glazed and his hand was wrought numb, and he fell to his knees in wonder. For he had never been so treated by a doughnut before, and he was sore amazed. And he said to the doughnut, "Wherefore do you chastise me concerning my mother, whom I do not know? And if she is in the basement, why has she never spake to me?" Whereupon God answered from the voice of the jelly glazed, saying, "Verily your mother is in the basement and you should do something about it." Whereupon the jelly glazed vanished and God spake no more. So Norris hauled himself up by his fat thighs and hastened to the basement, which he found to be locked. Norris fell down weeping in frustration, until a shining angel appeared before him, and the angel said, "Norris, fear not. For I am the angel Anthony, and I have brought the key to the basement door." And Norris fell down in wonder as the shining angel unlocked the door, and Norris entered the basement in great fear and trembling. The angel vanished at once. In the basement he found a beefy, chunky woman in chains and he fell at her knees and said, "Are you my mother, the fair Edna?" And Edna wept with joy at the sight of her son, and bathed his feet with her hair, and trimmed his nose hairs with a pair of clippers she carried in her skirt.

(*Silence.*)

PAUL. What a touching story.

J. It's actually not finished yet. I'm just getting my breath. (*Breathes.*) So Norris returned to his father, Nathan, and asked, "Father. Why do you have my mother chained steadfastly in the basement and why do you refuse to make her your legitimate full-fledged wife?" And Nathan answered, "The fair Naomi was my wife, whom I slew in a terrible rage, and I shall never have another. And your mother is a slough-pot of foulness." At which Norris became enraged and raised his hand to strike his father. But because he was fat and weak, the blow had no effect, and thereafter Nathan slew his son in a great rage. And then he ran to Edna and fell weeping at her feet and said, "Forgive me Edna, for I have slain our son in a great rage when he raised his hand against me." And Edna was sore with sorrow and cradled the head of Nathan and said, "Foul is your house with a great foulness, Nathan of Bermuda. We are accursed of God." And Nathan freed Edna, and gave her some money, and sent her to his cousin in Pasadena. And so Nathan descended into old age and slumber, with his father dead and the vineyards bearing less fruit than in his youth. And he was thankful for this time of peaceful contentment that had come to him in his old age. Till finally one day into his courtyard walked a young man bearing a cage in which a lizard sat.

PAUL. Again, the reptile.

J. And the lizard was calmly eating flies and watching Nathan, and the young man was very beautiful, and his name was Rodney. And Rodney said, "I come from your beautiful wife, Naomi, in the Land of the Place beyond the River, and she sends you greetings and asks that you accept this Lizard as a token of her affection, and that you feed it all your life, flies and other insects and whatever else you may find that pleases the Reptile, for this Reptile is the Son of God, born of the Outcast in the desert heat, and He has come to die for the sins of the world." Nathan accepted the lizard with great reverence and did as he had been asked to do. The lizard grew and waxed in sheen and glory and appearance of ancient wisdom.

PAUL (*after he realizes* J. *has stopped*). Go on.

J. That's it.

PAUL. What happened to the lizard?

J. Nothing.

PAUL. I don't understand.

J. The lizard is a figure in a parable. Nothing happens to figures in parables, actually. They are just figures. In parables.

PAUL. Whereas the lizard on the wall outside . . .

J. Is simply a lizard. Doing what lizards do. Without regard for our current religious crisis.

PAUL. I shall have to think about this.

(*Enter* SOL HEIFFER, *with* PAUL's *prayer cloth.*)

PAUL (*noting her presence*). Is it time already? (*With an air of grave responsibility, taking the prayer cloth in the beginning gesture of*

a somewhat smug ritual; to J.) This is the hour of prayer. The
hour when the humble kneel and bow their heads in the presence of the Almighty, subjugating themselves to the power of
the Father in the name of the Son in the presence of the Holy
Shadow. You will forgive me if I pray here, before you, in order
to save time.

J. As you wish.

PAUL. I feel so privileged doing this in front of you. And yet, at the
same time, so self-conscious.

J. There's no reason to be shy.

> (*Exit* SOL HEIFFER.
> *She returns immediately with a cassette recorder and a
> tray covered with a cloth.*
> *She waits quietly, holding the objects.*
> *The dialogue does not pause for her movement.*
> *If necessary she may make separate trips offstage to re-
> trieve these objects.*
> PAUL *does not note her presence until so noted in the
> stage directions.*)

PAUL. Perhaps I shall pray silently today. Usually I pray aloud and
record the prayer electronically. These prayers are transcribed
and published in quarterly volumes as *Paul's Daily Walks in the
Garden* and they do very nicely. Sales have declined somewhat
from an astonishing postwar peak. Not a sharp decline; a mod-
erate, tapering sort of decline which could probably be reversed
if I were to agree to another world tour. (*Pause.*) At any rate, I
could, today, pray silently and forgo the usual procedure.

J. I wouldn't be disturbed if you pray aloud.

PAUL. Perhaps I should pray aloud but simply pray a very innocu-
ous sort of prayer.

J. That doesn't sound like the ticket to me.

PAUL. No. It sounds rather like a sort of prayer consommé.

J. You should simply go on as if you were in your own private prayer chapel with the usual microphone in front of you.

PAUL. I suppose that is the only realistic choice. (*Notices* SOL HEIFFER *holding the tray; recognizes the tray and shudders.*) Oh no, Sol Heiffer. I couldn't possibly do that.

   (SOL HEIFFER *smiles beatifically.*)

J. (*to* PAUL). Are you all right?

PAUL (*gesturing to the tray*). No. I couldn't possibly. Do you know what that is?

J. I expect it's a sacramental service.

PAUL. I ordinarily take the Sacrament at the beginning of the hour of prayer.

J. Again, I must encourage you to follow through with all your usual procedures.

PAUL (*somewhat horror-struck*). But I simply cannot. There is no question. I can't be eating of your body and drinking of your blood right in front of you. That's simply out of the question. (*Signals* SOL HEIFFER *unequivocally to exit with the sacramental tray.*) The thought of the transubstantiation occurring right before your very eyes.

J. I find the possibilities to be somewhat interesting.

PAUL (*unrolling a prayer rug*). My knees aren't what they used to be.

   (PAUL *does brief vocal warmup.*)

PAUL. There. Now I feel relaxed. (*Pause. Closes his eyes and clasps his hands, then opens his eyes and speaks to* J.) I would prefer that you didn't begin answering my prayer till I get through the whole thing. Context, you know.

J. Of course. Whatever you like.

PAUL (*relieved*). Our Father, in the name of the Son, I beseech you. This is only a test. I beseech you yea verily in the name of the swan, the duck and the bone. This is only a test.

> (*In the prayer kit are a can of Sterno; a ritual stand on which to burn the Sterno; a silver or stainless steel plate; cash; a copy of the* Wall Street Journal; *a fertility goddess, a candy bar; and a cassette recorder, which* SOL HEIFFER *operates.*
>
> *Silently* PAUL *arranges the ritual objects downstage of the prayer rug.*
>
> SOL HEIFFER *holds the prayer kit while* PAUL *removes the objects one at a time.*
>
> *He first places the can of Sterno, unlit but ready for ignition, on the ritual stand, and places the stainless steel or silver plate next to the stand.*
>
> *Next he places the fertility goddess in front of the can of Sterno, facing the audience.*
>
> *He lays the* Wall Street Journal *at his right hand and the candy bar at his left hand, then lights the Sterno.*
>
> *Taking the whole stack of cash in his right hand and pulling off single bills crisply in his left,* PAUL *begins the prayer.*
>
> *He holds the cash, one bill at a time, over the Sterno flame and lets it burn.*
>
> PAUL *holds each bill as long as possible as it burns, then places the remnant in the silver plate, letting it burn on if God so pleases.*
>
> *When he has burned three bills, he reaches for the* Wall

Street Journal *without looking at it and waves it up*
and down, slowly, three times, lowering it to his
right again and returning to the burning of cash.
Then he begins the prayer.
When PAUL *begins the spoken prayer, he should reach*
over as part of the ritual and turn on the cassette
recorder.)

PAUL. O Father, God of the patriarchs, hear our humble prayer. We beseech you and most humbly invoke you. We turn to you with our whole hearts and our whole minds, open to you and quivering in anticipation of your divine presence. We are filled with love and a rich sense of nostalgia at this time. A warm spirit of brotherhood has come upon us on this wonderful day which you have created. We know in our hearts that we are blessed, and we declare before the world that you are a good God, a great God, and we are unworthy of you in any way, absolutely. Without question we are as the dust of your dust. You are over us as the sun is in the sky. Without you we would be less than the mustard seed, for we are filled with sin from the moment of our conception in our mother's womb, and we are foul and black with loathsome crawling oozing superating vile ulcerated cankerous sin till the day of our miserable death when worms and maggots will nest in our flesh and consume this worthless temple of sin in time's embrace. You are the Almighty God of Jerusalem and we are the vermin whom you have chosen, through your infinite grace, to love and cherish as if we were worthy of such a sublime emotion. We whose spirits are troubled within a burden of flesh. Not to mention my own slight infirmity. For we are humble and you are great. And so in humility I approach thee in prayer. I pray and beseech you, be good to the weak and the afflicted, and strike down the strong and the mighty where they be unworthy of the great rewards you have heaped upon them. And bring blessedness to the widows, the orphans, the poor and the suffering. Have mercy upon us, now that you have sent your shepherd to live among us, and let him afflict us not with too much revelation. Teach us the truth as we are able to receive it and not all at once in a rush so that we are apt to forget big chunks. Bring peace abroad to all peoples and here in our city as well, from neighbor to neighbor and kind to kind. Above all, work out your own will among us, and teach us to live more as you would have us live. For me, I would ask only that you help me to get the deposition I need to convince my adversaries within the church that I am the cornerstone of your church and of your message in this world. Please reveal to me this revelation for which I have waited and yearned through all these ages. Please let me hear the words that will teach me faith in my own salvation, after such a long career. In the name of You-Know-Who I pray. Amen.

> (*At the end of the prayer,* PAUL *eats the candy bar, chewing serenely and gazing into the audience.*
>
> *During the prayer itself,* SOL HEIFFER *stands attentively just behind* PAUL.
>
> *Toward the end of the prayer,* J. *gets her attention.*
>
> *He produces an object wrapped in wax paper from his robe and signals that he wants to give this object to* SOL HEIFFER *secretly.*
>
> SOL HEIFFER *signals that she wants to know what it is.*
>
> J. *signals in some manner that it is her tongue and repeats this when* SOL HEIFFER *cannot believe him.*

SOL HEIFFER *takes the package, opens it quietly.*

The audience should glimpse the fleshy object.

J. *indicates that it is a peel-and-stick tongue that she has only to put in place.*

SOL HEIFFER *mimics his gestures of instruction.*

By the time she turns her back on the audience to put the tongue in place, PAUL *should be eating the candy bar.*

She drops the bloody paper on the floor and makes a series of convulsive gestures.

There is a bright flash of light.

She turns, and her fingers are bloody.

She looks at J. *in amazement.*

PAUL *rises, licking his fingers after the candy bar.*)

SOL HEIFFER (*holding out her hands toward* PAUL). It's a miracle. Look.

      (PAUL *freezes.*

      If an intermission is deemed necessary, it should occur here, and the stage should go to black.

      If no intermission is employed, no blackout is needed.)

J. I thought your prayer was very touching.

PAUL. She spoke.

SOL HEIFFER. Yes I did.

PAUL. What happened?

J. I healed her.

PAUL. Just now?

J. Yes.

SOL HEIFFER. It's a miracle. See? (*Sticks out her tongue.*)

PAUL. Yes. Yes my dear, it certainly is. (*Examines her mouth, pats her on the head.*) Isn't that wonderful.

SOL HEIFFER (*pointing at* J.). He did it. He's terrific.

PAUL. He certainly is, isn't he?

SOL HEIFFER. It was in wax paper. My tongue was. And it was a peel-and-stick. See? (*Finds the peel-and-stick tab on the floor.*) You just peel. And stick.

PAUL. So I see. (*Pause.*) Now, go and gag yourself. Find a gag, or make one, and tie it round your head and through your mouth.

> (SOL HEIFFER *places the prayer objects back into the prayer kit.*
>
> *She may stay as long as necessary during the following, but should be offstage by the mention of "crippled and suffering martyrs."*)

J. You aren't reacting exactly as I expected.

PAUL. You don't seem to grasp the subtle implications of your capricious behavior.

J. Capricious?

PAUL. Yes, absolutely. Sol Heiffer is one of the great religious symbols of our time, and now you have ruined her. When she could not talk she had great significance. Her usefulness on posters and in brochures alone was fabulous, a real cornerstone of divine inspiration. Wise and holy through her silence. But now. In words she will destroy herself. Reduce her significance to naught. Inspire no one. When she speaks she will seem just like everybody else. A tedious bag of ailments and rheumy thoughts. Lacking that mystery with which we have so carefully surrounded her.

J. I thought you would be pleased. That her voice was restored.

PAUL. Of course, I do not question your wisdom in choosing to do as you have done. That would be totally inappropriate, and I would simply like to declare my faith that you have performed this miracle with the inscrutable majesty of divine will, inexplicable and all knowing, moving as it moves, without explanation or conceit. (*Pause.*) We will somehow adjust to this abrupt change in the status of one of our best crippled and suffering martyrs.

J. I expect you could rip her tongue out again, if you like.

PAUL. What do you mean, "again"? I did not rip out her tongue in the first place.

J. Pardon me. A slip of the tongue on my part. As it were. Anyway, I'm sure she would agree to the procedure. Provided you use the proper anesthetic technique. (*Pause.*) Or perhaps without anesthesia at all. I suppose there are people who enjoy that sort of suffering.

PAUL. Like nails, tearing through the flesh and bone of the hand.

J. The innocent hand.

PAUL. Yes. Innocent, by all means. If only I had been there to see it.

J. I could tell you about worse. Horrible tortures. Agonies beyond belief. Infinite crucifixions within the tormented physical recesses of black-hole singularities. Bringing salvation wherever it was needed across the whole expanding cosmos, my Father's idea of a joke, I suppose.

PAUL. I couldn't possibly have her tongue torn out.

J. I'm not entirely convinced by your tone.

PAUL. No, really. It would be beyond my power. My sense of justice or charity. Above all, charity. Which is of course a polite term for love, the love of one being for another. No, I love Sol Heiffer far too much to order her tongue ripped out by the roots, savagely. I love her for so many important reasons that it would be hard to prioritize them. No, I could not order such an act.

J. At any rate, to change the subject, I did find your prayer to be very touching.

PAUL. Coming from you, I take that as a great compliment.

> (*Crowd noise erupts with great violence, much closer this time.*
>
> *Enter* SOL HEIFFER, *gagged but obviously bursting with news.*)

PAUL (*to* J.). What are they doing now?

J. I really don't have the slightest idea.

> (SOL HEIFFER *makes it obvious that she knows.*)

PAUL (*to* SOL). Go and get me a report. From anyone you can find.

> (SOL HEIFFER *motions to the gag and offers to give the report herself.*)

J. She could tell us herself, you know.

PAUL. She? Her?

J. Yes.

PAUL. Apparently she has caught a glimpse of something. (*Pause.*) But it would never do. Would it? No. It is better for women not to speak.

> (*The crowd noise continues until indicated.*
>
> *Sounds of demolition, stone crashing, glass breaking.*)

J. I think we should listen to her.

PAUL. Naturally one would suspect so. But let us examine this thesis of yours more closely. What leads you to this supposition? Her eager manner, that's what. Her overwhelming enthusiasm at the prospect that she herself might be the messenger whose news sets into motion certain awesome events. Here she's only had her tongue back ten minutes or so and already she's blabbing gossip into every listening ear.

J. Actually she doesn't have her old tongue back. This is a brand-new tongue.

(SOL HEIFFER *is somewhat shocked by this news.*)

PAUL. Whatever the case. There's something undeniably cloying about her behavior. This is the nature of women, of course. Whatever she has seen, she would corrupt with her testimony. By the fact of her nature. No, it's better that women should not speak. Words will get her nowhere. Only in the purity of her suffering silence was she near the divine mystery of her true being.

J. (*to* SOL HEIFFER). You really should object to this sort of wholesale characterization.

PAUL. For the good of her soul I cannot allow even that much speech on her part.

J. (*to* PAUL). I don't think it's very wise of you to take that tone with me.

PAUL. She is my servant, my obedient flock member, one who turns to me for guidance. (*To* SOL HEIFFER.) I'm sorry to chastise you so, servant of God. But you have always found my advice to be beneficial to you in the past. (*Sighs.*) I can't order someone to rip your tongue out again for you. That would be wrong of me. But I can say, sincerely, with all my heart, that you ought to rip out your tongue yourself, immediately, for your own good. Do it now, do it in this room. Get a little enamel pan to catch the blood. But for the sake of your immortal soul, Sol Heiffer, you must not speak. It is better that you keep silence. Even about what you have just seen.

(SOL HEIFFER *looks at* J.)

J. I can't replace it again if you do. Maybe if you rip off a breast or something, I could help you.

PAUL. A breast? (*Laughs.*) That would hardly be sufficient when it is silence that you so desperately need, and not a flat chest. Again, Sol Heiffer, I cannot compel you. It would be wrong for me to exercise undue influence in this matter. But I believe it to be of the utmost importance. To the salvation of your (we hope) immortal soul. Not to mention its trickle-down effect on our organization, for we would simply have no further use for you if you could speak. Even the story of your miraculous healing would not suffice to repay us for the investment we have in your ongoing suffering. You should think primarily of the salvation of your own soul and secondarily of the good of the organization to which you owe so much. And you should rip out your tongue at once.

J. By way of compromise, may I offer an alternative?

PAUL. I don't see how any alternative could be sufficient.

J. Now this is interesting. Don't you think it a little cheeky on your part to dispute with me in a matter of theology. Clearly if I am the one who is presenting the compromise, it must be sufficient to the cause.

PAUL. This makes me extremely uncomfortable, your pulling rank on me like this.

J. I'm sorry to upset you, really, but I can't allow my position to erode any further than it has already.

PAUL. What are you suggesting?

J. Well, I think it's very simple. You have as your objective the preservation of this woman's silence as a resource for the edification of others. She, for her part, is delighted at the advent of this perfectly legitimate miracle which has restored her voice. A voice which has not been lifted to the praise of God in such a long time. And I am sure this poor voiceless woman longs to spend a minimum of a day in prayer before she rips her tongue out once again. I sense her longing for just exactly this sort of arrangement. Am I describing your fondest wishes, Sol Heiffer?

(SOL HEIFFER *nods somewhat hesitantly.*)

PAUL. This seems to me a very dubious proposition.

J. And, as an extra bonus, she could tell us what's happening outside.

PAUL. Your compromise proposition has great appeal to me and I will give it every consideration. But I'm afraid it's just out of the question. You have no idea. The havoc such a situation would wreak. Women speaking openly of their feelings and concerns at every sort of public gathering. The destruction of logic and reason. Chaos, in short. No. We will have information presented to us by a male adequately trained to such testimony.

(SOL HEIFFER, *hesitant at first, removes the gag.*)

SOL HEIFFER. There isn't anybody in the building. To report.

PAUL. So you fully intend to defy me and speak in my presence.

SOL HEIFFER. I just thought you would want to know that a lot of people have deserted the building. A lot of people. They've gone outside to dance with the strangers.

PAUL. Dance?

SOL HEIFFER. Outside. With those people in the courtyard.

PAUL. Everyone is gone? They're dancing? But I didn't hear any music.

(SOL HEIFFER *and* J. *look at each other.*)

SOL HEIFFER (*after a moment, lying*). There wasn't any music. They were just dancing.

PAUL. Are you sure?

SOL HEIFFER. I saw them. I watched.

PAUL. And you yourself heard no music. And you are hearing no music now.

SOL HEIFFER. No.

PAUL (*to* J.). And you? You also hear no music.

J. It would be impossible to speculate.

PAUL. Then you do hear something.

J. If there was dancing, it is very likely that I heard the dancing. The music that was inherent in the dancing, the rhythmic shuffling of feet over the flagstones of the courtyard. The low hum with which most people pass the day, the repetition of some bland tune from radio. Multiplied by all the hundreds, possibly thousands.

SOL HEIFFER. Thousands. Definitely.

PAUL (*to* J.). This is what you told them to do when you were in the market.

J. I don't recall demonstrating any dance steps on the melon cart.

PAUL. Don't ridicule me. This is what you have been planning all along. The total disruption of my activities. You are attempting to destroy me. I should have foreseen it.

SOL HEIFFER. They weren't destroying anything.

PAUL. Be quiet. How many people do we have left?

SOL HEIFFER. Some. I can't count.

PAUL. Any guards? Any carpenters?

SOL HEIFFER. I saw old Joseph, he's still here.

PAUL. Find him. Tell him to start building a cross.

SOL HEIFFER. Yes sir.

PAUL. Then bring me a ladder. Long enough to reach the window.

(*Exit* SOL HEIFFER.)

PAUL. I suppose now is as good a time as any.

J. Exactly what do you have in mind?

PAUL. I think you know. You leave me no choice. Actually.

J. I see.

PAUL. This is far earlier than I had planned.

J. I'm sure.

PAUL. Really. I was telling you the truth. About the pamphlets, the long peaceful interval in prison. The tasteful crucifixion in the fall. But you've left me no choice.

J. I hope you understand if I don't feel terribly forgiving.

PAUL. It was never my wish to cause you suffering. (*Pause.*) I know you don't believe that. I know you think I've had this in mind all along. But I truly wanted something else to happen. I wanted you to teach me this time. I wanted to hear words from your lips that would change my life.

J. You don't really have any idea what you wanted.

PAUL. Oh no. You've got it all wrong. I loved you. I still do. With all my heart. As sinners have loved saviors from the beginning of time.

> (*Enter* SOL HEIFFER, *with a ladder long enough to reach the window.*
>
> *She sets it against the wall.*
>
> *The conversation between* PAUL *and* J. *continues without pause.*
>
> *The crowd noise continues at varying levels, always present.*
>
> *To that sound is added the sound of hammers and nails.*)

J. You want salvation.

PAUL. Yes.

> (J. *laughs softly.*)

PAUL. It isn't funny.

J. (*still laughing*). Please.

PAUL. I will not be laughed at.

J. (*controlling himself*). Salvation. You. Really.

PAUL. Why is that so hard to believe?

J. Because it's you. Because you know how this game is played. But you want salvation anyway. It's too precious.

PAUL. Stop this.

J. Which kind do you want? The mansion in heaven and all that? Streets paved with gold? Choirs of angels? A bloody sheep sitting next to the right hand of God?

PAUL (*near rage*). Stop making fun of me! (*Pause.*) What did you tell the people in the market?

J. Why would I make fun of you?

PAUL. Answer me. Now.

> (*Silence suddenly.*
>
> *All crowd sound ceases.*
>
> *Hammers and nails fall silent.*)

J. I told them there is no God.

PAUL. What?

J. In the market. That's what I told them. Coming from me, it was a surprise.

PAUL. You must be joking.

J. No.

PAUL. Why would you tell them that?

J. It's true.

PAUL. Of course it isn't true. There is a God and you know that better than anybody; he's your Father.

J. My Father is dead.

PAUL. Is . . .

J. Dead. Didn't I tell you?

PAUL. No. (*Finding a place to sit down.*) It's a fairly significant omission.

J. It appears he may have been dead for some time and we simply haven't noticed. To the degree that such terms as "for some time" and "dead" are helpful when one is discussing my Father. (*Pause.*) So I told the people in the market that there is no God. Currently. Speaking in a purely local sense.

PAUL. And so they've stormed the walls. And now they will destroy the church.

J. Why would they do that?

PAUL. What is a church without God?

J. (*laughs, then speaks*). Then I told them they could bring him back. Only they. Not you, not your friends, not me, not my disciples, not the preacher, the pope or the politician. Nobody but them. By sacrifice. By finding just the right one. Together. In unison.

PAUL (*to* SOL HEIFFER). Climb the ladder and see what they're doing.

> (SOL HEIFFER *attempts to do so during the following exchange.*
>
> *The weight of the Bible, which she is still dragging, prevents her from climbing very high.*
>
> J. *continues without pause.*)

J. I can tell you what they're doing. They're searching for something in the courtyard. Silently, because they're all listening to each other. Breath and heart and everything. They figured out it was here pretty quick, the thing they were looking for, the thing they had to crucify. They figured there was nowhere else to put it. But here. Somewhere in your house. (*Pause.*) So I would like to talk to you about your salvation.

PAUL (*to* SOL HEIFFER). Aren't you there yet?

SOL HEIFFER. I never climbed anything before, I'm sorry.

J. You know, you'd have an easier time if you'd unchain yourself from that big book.

SOL HEIFFER. But that's the Holy Bible.

J. The what?

>   (SOL HEIFFER *just looks at him.*)

PAUL. It's the Bible.

J. What's that?

SOL HEIFFER (*to* PAUL). He doesn't know what the Bible is!

PAUL (*to* SOL HEIFFER). Never mind. (*To* J.) It's a collection of religious writings we put together a few hundred years after you died. Ascended, rather.

J. (*to* PAUL). Rather. (*To* SOL HEIFFER.) Take it off, Sol Heiffer. It's just dead weight.

>   (SOL HEIFFER *obeys but embraces the Bible after she has removed the chain. This should be done on the ladder.*
>
>   *They freeze into a tableau.*
>
>   SOL HEIFFER *standing on the ladder adoring the Bible should be specially illuminated with dime-store watercolor angel light.*
>
>   J. *addresses the audience directly, as if he has been doing so throughout.*)

J. We hope that the following moment will not strike anyone as irreverent.

>   (*Tableau breaks, light returns to its pretableau state.*
>
>   SOL HEIFFER *drops the Bible.*
>
>   *Laughs when it hits the floor.*)

SOL HEIFFER. I feel so light.

>   (J. *picks up the Bible and examines the table of contents.*
>
>   PAUL *is nervous as he does so.*)

PAUL. I've explained the sort of doctrinal problems we ran into in the absence of any written teachings. I think we did a pretty good job of coping. (*Nodding to the Bible.*) The book came out rather nicely. We picked the very best stuff, the really inspired writing.

J. I see a number of your letters made the cut.

PAUL. Yes, I was very fortunate in the selection process.

J. No doubt.

PAUL. No one was more surprised than I. And honored of course. Deeply honored. (*To* SOL HEIFFER.) Now climb to the window as I have requested.

> (SOL HEIFFER *does so.*
> *Light through the window changes, becomes blinding desert miracle light.*
> *Sound cue indicates that this is another miracle.*)

SOL HEIFFER. I see a bright light.

PAUL. That's the sun you idiot.

SOL HEIFFER. I see a hot desert. There's a whole lot of it and it looks real, like, scorching.

PAUL (*patiently*). I want to know what is happening in the court-yard.

SOL HEIFFER. You can't see the courtyard from this window, you can just see the desert.

J. Do you see anything else?

SOL HEIFFER. There's a road. And some rocks. And there's a car parked beside the rocks. And everything's really wavy from this shimmering stuff in the air. From the heat. And there's sky. Blinding blue sky.

J. Is there anyone in the car?

SOL HEIFFER. I think so. I see some arms inside. Maybe. But it's pretty far away.

J. Where does this road go? Do you know?

SOL HEIFFER (*studying the road and then smiling*). This is the road to Damascus. I've seen it before.

PAUL. You can't see the Damascus road from that window. Come down from there. Now.

> (SOL HEIFFER *studies the scene through the window*
> *another moment and then descends quickly.*
> *As soon as she is free of the ladder,* PAUL *ascends.*
> J. *does not hold for any of this but speaks over the action.*
> *When* PAUL *reaches the top of the ladder, the light*
> *through the window goes to a dark, God-in-the-*
> *thunderclouds kind of light.*
> *The miracle sound cue is repeated.*)

J. Perhaps you should let her stay there. Maybe she could give you your deposition if she watches. An eyewitness account. From years after the event, of course, but the law is a strange mistress. Perhaps she could get pictures of the miracle over the desert. Maybe even videotape. Documentation.

PAUL. I can't see anything.

SOL HEIFFER. Sure you can, there's all this sand.

PAUL. There's no sand, there's no road. There's no courtyard. There's nothing. Everything is dark. (*To* J.) Why won't you show me anything?

> (*Silence.*
> PAUL *continues to study what he sees through the*
> *window.*
> *His focus should remain there and only occasionally*
> *on* J.)

J. As I was saying. I would like to talk to you about your salvation.

PAUL (*after a moment*). What do you want to know?

J. I want you to tell me, what do you believe?

PAUL (*looking out the window through the whole speech*). That you are the Son of God. That you died and rose again. That because you did, I can. That you went to heaven to prepare a place for us. That you will return one day—and so you have —to take us home with you.

J. (*still holding the Bible, now in some way emphasizing its thickness*). That's it?

PAUL. Yes.

J. That's all this book says?

PAUL. There was some elaboration of the message.

J. (*placing the book on the floor*). Do you believe what you just said?

PAUL. Yes.

J. Do you believe in me?

PAUL (*without conviction*). Of course I do.

J. Then come and worship me.

> (*Silence.*
> PAUL'*s focus shifts away from the window.*)

PAUL. Excuse me?

J. If you believe in me as your salvation, come and worship me. Now.

> (*Silence.*)

PAUL. What would you like me to do?

J. Kneel. Let your soul pour forth adoration. For me. Verbal adoration. Fervently spoken. Now.

PAUL. Are you serious?

J. More than that. I'm divine.

> (*After brief hesitation,* PAUL *descends the ladder.*
> *At the foot of the ladder, he stops.*)

PAUL. Kneel and . . .

J. Worship me.

(PAUL *slowly kneels and grasps the hem of* J.'s *garment.*
He is never resolved to the action, however.
He freezes.)

PAUL. I can't do this.

J. It isn't so much I'm asking. A few moments of affection. A little
sacrifice on your part.

(*Nevertheless* PAUL *slowly stands.*)

PAUL. I'm terribly sorry.

J. (*sighing*). I've done all I can do.

PAUL. I'll worship you later. After all this other business is finished.

J. Yes of course.

PAUL. Meantime we have this business at hand. The sacrifice of
which you spoke.

J. Don't you want your deposition?

PAUL (*lowering his voice*). You mean, you're willing to give it?

J. Yes, of course.

PAUL (*overcome*). Thank you. I can't tell you how much. How grate-
ful. (*To* SOL HEIFFER.) Is my tape recorder still here?

SOL HEIFFER (*finding and bringing it*). Yes sir.

PAUL (*to* J.). My attorney wanted to be present. To ask the questions. But I suppose he isn't presently available.

J. I would be happy to wait.

(*Crowd sound returns.*)

PAUL. We can't. (*Listens to the mob, which is moving restlessly out-*
side, like a crowd at intermission.) Yes, I suppose we should get
that under way too. (*To* SOL HEIFFER.) Go and find the captain
of the guard. Tell him I will need him to escort the prisoner to
the courtyard.

SOL HEIFFER. Him?

PAUL. Yes.

SOL HEIFFER. Now?

J. It's all right, Sol Heiffer.

PAUL. We have no choice in the matter. Now, please go and do as I asked.

>(*Exit* SOL HEIFFER.

>PAUL *gets the tape recorder and checks for a tape.*)

PAUL. This is generous of you, given the circumstances. I might have expected worse.

J. It's really nothing. Chalk it up to my infinite good nature.

PAUL. Oh no, it's a greater favor than I can explain. I might have lost everything. All I've worked for—we've worked for—centuries of labor—down the tube. Zip. Because I had no pictures, no autograph, no lock of your hair. As if I could have remembered to ask for such a thing. When you had taken the trouble to appear to me miraculously in the middle of nowhere.

J. With so few witnesses.

PAUL. Exactly. Of course, I would have preferred a more public miracle, of the sort you used to do in your heyday, walking on the water and feeding the multitude, that sort of thing. But what you gave me in the desert was terrific. More than I deserved. Even now, so many years afterward, I blush to remember how innocent I was before that blinding moment. Before you shed your grace on me. Before I realized my absolute love for you and took up my world mission.

J. Actually, only one other person ever loved me so completely or absolutely.

PAUL. John, of course.

J. No. Judas. He also loved me enough to have me killed.

PAUL. I don't think that's fair.

>(J. *laughs, softly*)

PAUL. No, really. I don't appreciate the comparison.

J. (*still laughing; controlling himself*). All right. All right. Let's get on with your deposition. Will you be questioning me yourself, then?

PAUL. Perhaps you could simply recount the events of the day as you remember them.

J. Day?

PAUL. When you appeared to me. In the desert.

J. From my point of view there was no day.

PAUL. I beg your pardon.

J. Or night. (*Smiles.*) Day has meaning for you because you are confined to it. But I am not, for the most part. So that, whenever it was I appeared to you, however long ago it was, I simply entered your local space-time and established some moments of three-dimensional duration within the ten or eleven oscillating dimensions that constitute your reality. Your universe. My Father's little conundrum. So, you see, while from your point of view that was one event in a sequence, from my point of view it is simply one of many possible events placed within the continuum that I view as eternity. In other words, the miracle you describe undoubtedly does exist somewhere within the whole spectrum of events that are plausible and that are likely to have involved me. But it is extremely difficult, even for me, to locate specific events within the infinite range of possible occurrences. It is also rather dangerous.

PAUL. Please try. It was a Saturday night. A year or so after you died. I was restless. I had just bought a new car.

J. (*sighing*). Since you insist. (*Pause.*) You had waited till after Sabbath was over. The sun well down below the horizon. A partly cloudy night. You gassed up your Maserati and left the city by the postern gate. You traveled light. An overnight bag, a couple of paperbacks. Detective mysteries. Ninja novels. You were headed to Damascus to spend the weekend with your good friend Sarah Hofstein, an elderly librarian with interests in the arts.

> (*Early on in this speech, but not during the first sentence,* PAUL *turns on the tape recorder.*)

PAUL. I had no idea your memory was so detailed.

J. The word "memory" has very little application in this case. I am fully capable of imagining the event exactly as it occurred.

> (PAUL *shuts off the tape recorder.*)

PAUL. If I'm going to record this, you must not use words like "imagine."

J. But it's perfectly true.

PAUL. It's not helpful.

J. In fact, if I'm not careful, if I make a mistake during my remembering, the past will reorder itself to conform to my memory. This preserves my infallibility even as entropy increases.

PAUL. I'm about to turn this on again. Now remember, I was driving to Damascus.

> (*The effect, beginning about midspeech, should be that* PAUL *cannot quite place each detail as* J. *describes it.*
>
> *In fact,* J. *is lying about small details, but as he does so, the past rearranges itself to conform to his lie, and* PAUL's *memory changes after a moment's drag.*)

J. Troubled by recent memory. The feeling of blood on your hands. Even though you cannot historically be connected with the murder of Stephen, still, in your heart of hearts, you knew yourself to be directly responsible. Further persecutions were planned. You could not even name my twelve disciples at the time but you had vowed to eradicate them and furthermore to stamp out every trace of this new religious sect which you feared as a possible source of tension. So your mind was filled with images of murder as you drove through the midnight countryside. Spending the night at a cheap motel a couple of hours down the road. The mattress too hard, no little soap in the little soap dish, the glass on the steel shelf already unwrapped, grimy. The impossible heat beginning at sunrise. No air conditioner known to man could even cut it. You set out at dawn for Damascus. Delirious. Having had no breakfast, except a box of frosted Pop-Tarts from a local convenience store.

PAUL. I don't remember the part about the Pop-Tarts.

J. Grape-flavored. With white frosting. And a large black coffee with a little mouth-hole torn out of the plastic cover. Shifting the gears of the Maserati with one hand and opening Pop-Tarts with the other. The Damascus road was a breeze. You could steer with your knees. You opened all the windows, but the heat was relentless. The sun was scorching the tops of your arms and thighs.

> (*Crowd sound shifts from murmuring to something of a higher pitch.*)

PAUL. Please. It isn't necessary for you to remember what happened to me in such detail. Stick with what happened to you. When you appeared.

J. You weren't alone, were you? No. You weren't. (*Pause.*) Who was with you, Paul?

> (*Enter* SOL HEIFFER.
> *They look at her.*)

J. Did you suppose no one would ever find out?

PAUL (*attempting to shut off the tape recorder but finding he cannot*). Stop it. That's enough.

J. But that's not even the best part.

PAUL (*as if seeing a picture inside his head*). No one was with me. This is not how it happened.

J. One can never be certain. Do you feel your memory changing? Do you see the companion, now?

PAUL. You cannot possibly do this to me.

J. Sweet, soft and naive. Luminous in the seat next to you. Obedient and pliant to your will. You gather her in your arms, the Maserati still warm from its desert run, the hot sun on your back and on her thighs—

PAUL. This never happened. You know perfectly well I am incapable. My little infirmity.

J. But you remember her. Don't you? Of course you do. You were perfectly whole that afternoon. This was long before your legendary self-castration, which is, after all, disputed by most reputable sources. And you remember, as I describe, your companion's soft hair tangled in your lips. Your body spinning in a thousand directions, approaching infinity but still frightened. And then, as you were beginning your little act of self-abandon, over the desert a blinding light appeared, and you thought it was for you.

PAUL. This is not how it happened. I have never remembered it this way before.

J. This isn't how you wrote it down, is it?

PAUL. No. No.

J. Those documentation problems. Can be tricky. When your memory goes. How could you have forgotten the smell of her freshly washed hair? Or the light, when it first appeared, not white but amber. Glittering. And a deep voice that said, "Saul, Saul, why do you persecute me?" And you leaned up over the ecstatic, shuddering body of your companion, and you hid your face in your hands. But the light was too fierce, seeping through your closed fingers, prying open the lids of your eyes. And you opened your eyes. And your companion, beneath you, was no longer the woman who had ridden with you all that way through the desert. She was not a woman at all. Her skin was cold, white, scaly, her body stiff, her thick tail lashing beneath you. And you were plunged deep inside her, and God was watching. At last, mercifully, you were blind. But then the tongue of the lizard touched your throat, and you took it in your hands and ripped it free.

SOL HEIFFER (*touching a hand to her throat*). I remember.

PAUL. No. You appeared to me. You said, "Saul, Saul, why do you persecute me?" And I said. I said. I was looking at the light. (*Pause.*) And then Sam Jennings and Bert Bryant—

SOL HEIFFER. No. That's not the way it happened.

PAUL. You can't possibly know anything about it.

SOL HEIFFER. I remember. Sam and Bert came later. The next day. After.

(PAUL *focuses on* SOL HEIFFER *with a great effort.*)

PAUL. What are you talking about? I trust you have found the guard captain as I ordered.

SOL HEIFFER (*glancing at* J.). Yes sir.

PAUL. You're lying. Of course you are. You never went anywhere.

SOL HEIFFER. The guards will be here soon.

PAUL. There should be no reason for delay. Why can't they come now, at once, as I asked?

J. There's nothing to be afraid of.

PAUL (*throwing the cassette recorder against the wall; turning to* SOL
HEIFFER). Go and get them now. Tell them to come now.
>(*The crowd erupts, louder than at any point before.*
>*Exit* SOL HEIFFER.)

J. Foolish. Don't you think? The way they sound, all together. Like
animals at feeding.

PAUL. My attorney wouldn't have used it anyway. It wasn't a real
deposition.

J. That's right.

PAUL. My head will clear in a few days.

J. Maybe you should read your own account of what happened.
Sam Jennings and Bert Bryant, all that.

PAUL. You called me by name.

J. Yes. Yes, I suppose I did.

PAUL. Then you admit it. This whole game of yours. It's a sham.
My memories. Are false. The incident with the woman never
happened. You've tampered with me. Admit it.

J. (*quietly, simply*). I've told you the truth. Whatever I told you. Is
the truth. Now and forever. (*Pause.*) The woman in the desert
had a child. The child was a lizard. Nathan raised the child.
You remember Nathan, don't you? From my parable?

PAUL. I will not believe it.

J. Your old memories will fade. Only the new ones will remain.

PAUL. You had no right to tamper with my mind.

J. It wasn't your mind I changed. It was the past.
>(*Silence.*
>*The implications of this sink in.*
>PAUL *kneels in front of* J. *in a pose of worship and*
>*grasps the hem of* J.*'s robe.*)

PAUL. The Lord my God is a mighty God, he upholds the righteous

and casteth down those who do wickedness. In the strength of
the Lord my God I will stand, for you are a mighty rock, and
there are none who can come against you.

>   (*Enter* SOL HEIFFER, *with a cross on which is the figure
>   of a crucified lizard.*
>   *She leans the cross against the wall and takes her place
>   beneath it, the Mother of the Lizard, mourning
>   the sacrifice.*
>   *By the end of the speech,* PAUL*'s old memories are fading
>   fast.*)

PAUL. For you have sent your Son to die for the sins of the world,
and he is come among us with great righteousness, and light
shines from him as from the sun, and his glory is the glory of
your name, and his strength is the strength of your Word, and
his grace is the grace of the innocent. For he is without sin. And
behold, men have chastised him and vilely used him, and they
have raised him up to you, as a sacrifice to you, even your Son
whom you freely gave. But now the Mocker has come among
us. And he mocks at you with a great voice, and foulness issues
from his mouth. In no wise can he abide your tender mercy or
your loving truth. Behold, with his tongue he has brought a
great sin upon my house, for I mistook him for your Son and
brought him to live among my private chambers. But he has
lain among my innocent children like a poison. He came not
as once he came to me in the desert, with a blinding light and
gentle words. He has been among my followers like the pesti-
lence, and he has brought great evil to me and all my kind.

J. That's enough.

PAUL (*raising his head*). You're still here.

J. Yes.

PAUL. Will the guards come soon? You're to be crucified.

J. Yes. I know.

(*Silence.*)

PAUL. It isn't fair. What you've done.

J. It's dangerous. Worshiping an omnipotent God. You should have thought of that.

PAUL (*seeing* SOL HEIFFER). Sol. Sol Heiffer. What are you doing there?

SOL HEIFFER (*gesturing to the lizard*). My son is dead.

PAUL. I'm terribly sorry.

(SOL HEIFFER *reaches her hand toward* PAUL.)

SOL HEIFFER. He died on the cross.

PAUL. Yes. I can see.

SOL HEIFFER. Would you like to hear about him? About his immaculate conception? His childhood wisdom? His virtuous death? Would you like me to tell you the story?

PAUL (*joining her, laying his head in her lap*). Yes. But not now.

(*Lights down to form two pools of light onstage.*

One is on the crucifixion scene.

The other is on J., *who goes to the cot, kneels, and pulls a suitcase from beneath.*

Removing his robes, he folds them and puts them in the suitcase.

This leaves him in his underwear and sandals.

He puts on a man's business hat.)

J. Today. In the market. My message was simple. I said, enough. I said, I didn't come back for nice-guy stuff. Plowshares into swords, remember? That's what I said. You want to make religion work for you? Maybe you better just start over. You're in the holy city for the weekend? All right. Begin with that.

Tonight we're going to burn this city down. (*Laughs.*) I said that. (*Laughs; begins to exit with the suitcase.*) That's pretty good. Burn this city down.

> (*Stops at the foot of the cross for a moment of silence, at the end of which he bows his head politely.*)

J. Better you than me. O lizard of righteousness.

> (*Exit* J.
>
> *Lights to black a moment later, excepting only the eyes of the lizard, which continue to glow, the new sacrifice.*)

Kaye Gibbons, on *The Borderland*

Hardscrabble southerners, as remarkably portrayed in *The Borderland*, do not suffer interlopers from the city gladly. People such as Grimsley's Rollins couple critique and pass judgment on strangers who wonder how such people manage to back some semblance of life out of the tangled, violently composed wrecks of their existence. The Rollinses, in their favor, were born of the land and know their way through fields in the dark, and when we consider that southerners have forever loved land, we see that by owning a piece of the earth they are actually better southern citizens than the play's chief irritant, Gordon Hammond.

Grimsley writes of what happens when two diametrically opposed married couples breach the borderland, both physical and spiritual, that separates their lives. This tale of life roiling in a crucible has been acted out before, by Tennessee Williams, Edward Albee, and every writer who has looked for the extraordinary collision of cultures and values. Grimsley, however, transcends the bulk of modern fiction by blurring the dividing line a bit by his methods of characterization. He shows, always; he tells us only what we need to know and is then quiet. He is never a preacher, never didactic. But somehow at the play's end, we see in retrospect how he manages his shades of gray, how subtly his characters convey the heart of the story. We never feel that Grimsley has any animosity, any scores to settle. It is plain that he respects his art form, his language, too much to turn a fine story into a social diatribe. He certainly had the chance and was wise enough not to take it. He is interested in words, symbols, metaphor, and character. In all of Grimsley's work, there are those powerful characters, straining to break free from the page.

The Hammonds and the Rollinses live by different rules, treasure different ideals, if one can say that the wife-beating, violent-natured Jake has any ideals other than the solely utilitarian—eat, drink, procreate until the wife is spent. His counterpoint, Gordon Hammond, is skittish, possibly impotent, and, in contrast to Jake, can wield neither his pistol nor his penis satisfactorily. The menace each one provokes—Jake physically and verbally, Gordon emotionally—is played out in the dark. Here, Grimsley's work with darkness recalls the famous last lines of *The Glass Menagerie*. If one of *Borderland*'s men had a bit of what the other had, they might make decent husbands. But they have been molded by circumstance, not nature, and this acculturation makes each, in his own way, a son of a bitch seldom so artfully drawn in literature.

The wives, Helen Hammond and Eleanor Rollins, have in common the singular ability to feel pain. We readily see what strife the common lot of male humanity has put them through, the emotional if not physical hurts, the trauma of a furious fist, the refusal to create a family. Helen has come to the country to find a life that southern city people, latent boomers, increasingly wish to imagine their grandparents had. They build "new" farmhouses, buy "new" antiques. Missing in the South now, among these interlopers and in Helen's life, is the authenticity, the realness. She has surrounded herself with new things—things that a true countrywoman can see only in catalogs or in rare glimpses inside one of these new neighbor's homes. And when Eleanor, wet, beaten, and scared, runs from the elements, and above all from the element of nature that her husband represents, to the safe and warm home of a much-concerned Helen, the borderland is crossed. When Jake comes to find her and drag her home, where he is in control, the trespass is powered by inchoate anger, loathing, sheer criminal intent. Here, Grimsley executes the crisis of the story in a few deft strokes. His language, always loaded even in his novels, is now so heavily freighted with portent that the reader may need to stop a moment, as I did, to let the puny little human heart adapt itself to the speed and intensity with which Grimsley is now propelling us toward the final moments. The reader may find the ride to that last scene to be more than he or she bargained for. As always, Jim Grimsley gives good value for your dollar. We are blessed that he is one of the most hard-working, honest, and intelligent writers working today.

THE BORDERLAND

The Borderland premiered at Currican Theatre in New York in October 1994, in a production directed by Dean Gray, featuring Elisabeth Lewis Corley as Helen, Laurence Lau as Gordon, Sarah McCord as Eleanor, and David Van Pelt as Jake. Sets were by Rob Odorisio; costumes, by Jonathan Green; lighting, by Jack Mehler; and sound, by Michael Keck.

HELEN HAMMOND, a woman in her early thirties. She has decided
to stay at home full-time, since her husband can now support a
family on his salary alone, and plans to have her first child soon.
GORDON HAMMOND, a professional in his early thirties. He has re-
cently received a promotion that has allowed him to buy a new
house in the country but within fairly comfortable commuting
distance of metropolitan Atlanta.
ELEANOR ROLLINS, a rural housewife in her mid- to late twenties
JAKE ROLLINS, a rural laborer in his late twenties

SETTING

The interior of an upper-middle-class house built in the country
by city people and intended to resemble other rural buildings in
superficial ways while providing all the comforts of the metro-
polis. The stage is dominated by two large windows. Suggested
set pieces might be fake primitive woodwork and furniture, a
country-style hearth, anything of that sort, but nothing should
be overdone. The exits suggest the larger house surrounding the
stage. Beyond the windows is a porch, though this need not be
represented in any way, except that storm effects should be muted
by the porch. The play begins in late afternoon. Rigid adherence
to any period is neither necessary nor desirable. Storm effects
must be of high quality, since they pervade the action.

ACT 1

HELEN *is found at the largest of the windows, almost lost in the
curtains.*
Enter GORDON, *with a paper, which he begins to read.*
He speaks to HELEN *while not actually concentrating on her.*
The wind is blowing outside.

GORDON. How's it looking?

HELEN. Cloudy. Wind's blowing.

GORDON. Another storm?

HELEN. I think so.

GORDON. I hope it's not as bad as last night.

> (GORDON *watches* HELEN *for a moment.*)

GORDON. Come out of there. You look lost.

HELEN. I'm all right.

GORDON. Come out of there anyway.

HELEN. But I like it.

> (GORDON *sits with the paper.*
> *A moment passes.*)

GORDON. What did you do today?

HELEN. Repotted my ferns.

GORDON. Again?

HELEN. Yes. (*Pause.*) They weren't right. From before.

GORDON (*still not really interested, but talking*). You said you had
    some kind of meeting.

HELEN. Library club. I didn't go.

GORDON. Why not?

HELEN. I just didn't.

GORDON. I thought you liked those women.

HELEN. There's one man in the group.

GORDON. Really?

HELEN. He's very bright. He reads Spanish.

GORDON. But you still didn't go to the meeting, even to hear this
    man read Spanish.

HELEN. Why would he read Spanish at the meeting? (*Pause.*) I felt
    shy at the last minute. They've all known each other for years.

GORDON. I'm sure they like you fine.

HELEN. Anyway, I watched a good movie on TV.

    (*Silence.*)

GORDON (*looking entirely away from the paper for the first time*). I'm worried about you.

HELEN. Why? I'm fine.

GORDON. I thought you would be happy when you didn't have to work.

HELEN. Oh Gordon, I'm fine. I'll go to the meeting next week.

    (GORDON *returns to his newspaper.*)

HELEN. I saw that woman again.

GORDON. Who are you talking about?

HELEN. The woman I told you about. I did, I remember telling you. Who lives in the house next door.

GORDON. The white woman with all the washing machines on her porch? The one who has about sixty children.

HELEN. She has five children.

GORDON. Five's enough. Don't you think?

HELEN. She's younger than me. Did you know that?

GORDON. No.

HELEN. She is. And she has five children. (*Pause.*) I can't even imagine what that's like. If we had five children in the house. Now.

GORDON. Where did you see her?

HELEN. Running across the field. A few minutes ago, this side of the bridge.

GORDON. Running?

HELEN. Yes.

GORDON. Where?

HELEN. To the woods. I didn't see where.

GORDON. Maybe she's just getting exercise.

HELEN. Don't be silly.

GORDON. When did you get to be so fascinated with this woman?

> (HELEN *should be free of the window by now.*)

HELEN. Her husband was in the yard. The side yard. Watching her. Not chasing her. Just standing there.

GORDON. How do you know how old she is?

HELEN. I talked to her last week. At Mr. Jarman's store. I gave her a ride home.

GORDON. What made you do that?

HELEN. She had more than she could carry. One of the children was with her but he was too small to carry much. She shops at that store. Not like we do, not just when she's out of something, she buys all her groceries there.

GORDON. At those prices?

HELEN. She was planning to walk home with two heavy bags. And this sweet little boy trying to help her.

GORDON. This is really too much. You sound like a social worker.

HELEN. I knew you wouldn't like it. That's why I didn't tell you.

GORDON. She should learn to drive.

HELEN. She knows how to drive.

GORDON. There's a car right in the yard.

HELEN. I know. I suppose it doesn't work.

GORDON. Well I'm sure I've seen her husband in it. In motion.

HELEN. Well I didn't question her about it.

GORDON. She was probably lying. She probably can't drive at all. Too frightened to learn. Too stupid. Something like that.

HELEN. I don't think she's stupid.

GORDON. How do you know?

HELEN. Because I'm not stupid and I talked to her.

> (GORDON *goes to* HELEN, *who is still standing, and
> embraces her.*
> *She speaks past his shoulder.*)

HELEN. When I saw her running. Her face. She was so afraid. And there he was just standing there. I couldn't imagine what she could be running from.

GORDON. There could be a thousand reasons. You can't help her by trying to imagine them all.

HELEN. She's still out there somewhere. She hasn't gone back across the field.

GORDON. Come sit down.

HELEN. I'm all right.

GORDON. I don't think you are. Come on.

(GORDON *leads* HELEN *to a seat.*)

GORDON. Lean back. Lean back against me. That's good.

(*Sound of wind.*)

HELEN. Listen. Do you hear?

GORDON. We may have quite an evening.

HELEN. Is it getting darker?

GORDON. Hush. Be still. Relax, let me hold you.

(HELEN *gradually relaxes.*)

HELEN. I need to get supper.

GORDON. Relax for a minute. Now listen. Just listen. You cannot let yourself get involved with these people. If they have problems, they have to solve them. Without any help from you or me.

HELEN. I just gave her a ride home from the store, Gordon.

GORDON. That's not what I'm talking about. I'm talking about you. You're letting these people affect your mind.

HELEN. I just feel so bad, watching them. Their clothes. Their house. I wouldn't make a dog live in that house. People shouldn't have to live like that.

GORDON. I know they shouldn't. But people have been living like that forever. And there isn't a whole lot people like you and me can do about it.

HELEN. That sounds so simple when you say it.

GORDON. It is. Really. Listen, Mr. Jarman told me all about these people. He's known them for years. This is just the way they are, fighting all the time. This is just the way they live.

HELEN. I thought you didn't remember her.

GORDON. What?

HELEN. When I brought her up. I thought you didn't remember her.

GORDON. I didn't.

HELEN. Oh.

GORDON. Mr. Jarman started the conversation, not me. Way back when we moved in. He asked me if we liked our new neighbors, and I said I didn't know anything about them. And he said to keep it that way. He said their people have been living in shacks like that as far back as anybody can remember.

HELEN. Mr. Jarman doesn't know everything.

GORDON. He's been around here a lot longer than we have.

HELEN. That family wouldn't live that way if somebody would teach them better.

GORDON. How do you know? Do you know what to teach them?

HELEN. No.

GORDON. Then how do you know what to do?

HELEN. I just know. It makes sense. (*Pause.*) I know for sure that woman shouldn't have to be afraid of her husband.

GORDON (*gently, without condescension*). You don't know if she's afraid of him or not. And it doesn't matter anyway. The point is still the same. We can't do anything about the way they live. (*Pause.*) At least it's not like that for everybody. (*Pause.*) Now let me tell you a story about a man who loved his wife very much, see if that will make you feel better. Once upon a time there was a man who loved his wife very much. Almost as much as I love you. He had a good job and he worked very hard because he wanted to take care of his wife forever and ever. He bought her a fine house and bought her nice clothes, he gave her a car to drive and her own money to spend. He took her to church and to prayer meeting and they ate dinner at good places and whenever they were in public he kept her close to him and protected her. And he spent a lot of time thinking, all the time, of ways to make her happy and to make her life as easy and safe as it could be. Because he loved her. Because he had always loved her, ever since he first knew her. And he wanted her to be happy all the time and never have any worries at all. And he always treated her kindly and never chased her into the woods. Doesn't that sound like a nice story?

HELEN. It's very nice.

GORDON. Do you feel better?

HELEN. Yes. I'm fine.

> (HELEN *rises.*)

GORDON. What's wrong? What did I say?

HELEN. Nothing.

GORDON. Something's wrong, I can tell.

HELEN. Listen to you. You're making fun of me. Your story. It isn't even a story. Nothing happens. You give me money. You take care of me. You protect me. You make me happy. You love me. What do I do?

GORDON. I didn't mean anything like what you're making of it.

HELEN. No, tell me. What do I do? In your story. What do I do? (*Pause.*) I'll tell you what I do. I take care of the house. I thaw out chicken. I repot the ferns.

GORDON. That's not what I meant.

HELEN. I never should have let you talk me into this. I didn't get
   this angry at you when I was still working.

   (*Phone rings before she finishes.*

   GORDON *answers it.*

   HELEN *returns to the window.*)

GORDON. Hello Jenny. (*Looks at* HELEN, *who shakes her head no.*)
   No. She's not here right now. I don't know where she is. The
   car was gone when I got home. She'll be back sometime soon,
   she's never gone long. You want me to . . . (*Pause; looks for
   paper, then realizes he doesn't need to take a message.*) You want
   me to take a message? Sure, I'll get her to. Sure. Oh, she's fine.
   (*Pause.*) She didn't go? Well, I wonder why. I know she loved
   that book she was reading last week. (*Pause.*) Well, she's not
   sick, she's fine. (*Pause.*) Good. Say hello to Bob for me. Is he
   still fat as ever? Yeah? That's great. No, that's great. Yeah, sure.
   Take care too. Bye.

HELEN. She asked about the meeting.

GORDON. She was afraid you missed because you were sick.

HELEN. I'm supposed to take her some recipes tonight.

GORDON. Well, get your sweater and we'll run over there. It'd be
   nice to see big old Bob anyway.

HELEN (*looking out the window*). I don't want to go. Not right now.
   (*Pause.*) I'll call her in a few minutes.

   (GORDON *watches* HELEN.)

GORDON. Would you come away from there?

HELEN. I'm watching the clouds, that's all.

   (GORDON *comes up behind her and embraces her.
   She allows this but not with enthusiasm.*)

GORDON. I'm sorry. I didn't think of my story as making fun of
   you.

HELEN. It's all right.

GORDON. I guess in some ways this has been the hardest on you. Moving out here.

HELEN. It's fine, most of the time. I miss my job. (*Pause.*) That's so funny. I never thought I would.

GORDON. You'll feel different once you see Dr. Luder again. Once you know for sure you're pregnant. Then it won't seem like you don't have enough to do, then you'll have the baby to think about. (*Pause.*) You sure you don't want to go see old Bob and Jenny?

HELEN. I really don't feel like it tonight.

GORDON. Are you mad at her?

HELEN. No. I do get tired of her.

GORDON. I thought you liked her.

HELEN. I do. (*Pause.*) She bores me after a while. She's always making desserts. Tonight I'm supposed to take her a recipe for seven-layer pie. The one I can't stand, with all that canned lime juice on it. She'll probably make it while I'm sitting there and then feed half of it to Bob. (*Pause.*) I'd rather stay home. Where it's peaceful.

GORDON (*looking out the window*). If it stays peaceful. With this storm coming. (*Pause.*) Don't they ever plow cornstalks under?

HELEN. You're asking me?

GORDON. That field over there is so ugly, all those cornstalks and that mud. We should plant some trees at the edge of the yard.

HELEN. What about when it has corn in it? Didn't you want to watch the corn grow and all like that?

GORDON. We can go look at the corn when we want to go look at the corn. We'll walk out there and watch it. Stand under our trees and look at the corn. Like we were farmers.

HELEN. I went to see Dr. Luder today.

GORDON. You did? I didn't think the test would be back for another couple of days.

HELEN. The test isn't back yet. (*Pause.*) But my period started this morning. So I called him.

> (*Silence.*
>
> *Their disappointment indicates they have been trying to have a child for some time.*)

GORDON. So you're not pregnant.

HELEN. I guess I'm not. (*Pause.*) I was so sure this time.

GORDON. What did Luder say?

HELEN. He says you need to have a fertility test.

> (*Silence.*)

GORDON. So what you're saying is, this is my fault.

HELEN. No, that's not what I said and that's not what Dr. Luder said.

GORDON. Yes it is. You think there's something wrong with me, both of you.

HELEN. No, we don't.

GORDON. Then what do you want me to take some test for?

HELEN. There's nothing wrong with anybody. But there's some reason I'm not getting pregnant, Gordon. We're trying to find out what it is.

GORDON. How do you know it's not something wrong with you?

HELEN. I already had my tests. And I didn't make such a big deal about it, either.

GORDON. That's not the same thing.

HELEN. For goodness' sake, Gordon, of course it is. What is wrong with you?

GORDON. You have been at me about that test till I'm sick of it.

HELEN. Because we want to have a baby. Don't we?

GORDON. Yes.

HELEN. Have you changed your mind? Do you want to forget it?

GORDON. You know how much I want a baby.

HELEN. Well you have to do a little more about it than paint the nursery.

GORDON. Now that's not fair, I'm doing everything I can. We have just about beat each other to death trying to get you pregnant.

> (*Soft laughter.*
>
> *Silence.*)

HELEN. It's not anybody's fault.

GORDON. But you think it's because of me. Say it.

HELEN (*after a moment*). Yes. I guess I do.

> (*Silence.*
>
> GORDON *goes to the window.*)

HELEN. So will you please go to see Dr. Luder?

> (*Silence.*)

GORDON (*at the window*). There's your friend out there.

HELEN. Who? The woman?

GORDON. It looks like her husband. Trying to find his wife, I guess.

> (HELEN *joins him.*)

HELEN. I wonder why he's looking for her.

GORDON. Maybe he wants his supper.

HELEN. That's not funny. (*Turning away from the window.*) I ought to start yours. Ours.

GORDON (*gently; ending the argument without conceding*). You don't have to cook if you don't want to. We could get something in town. Have dinner at that home-cooking place.

HELEN. It's so far.

GORDON. I've gotten so I don't even think about driving, these days. If the traffic's not bad.

(*Wind rises suddenly.*

The sound of a screen door slowly banging is heard.)

HELEN. We don't want to go out in this.

GORDON. Honey, we'd be in a car.

HELEN. I hate driving in a storm. Especially on these narrow roads.

GORDON. I thought I fixed that goddamn door.

(*Exit* GORDON.

HELEN *opens the window, which should billow from breezes.*

The sound of the wind is closer.

She hears a smattering of rain.)

HELEN. That poor woman. That poor thing.

(*She steps away from the window.*

Enter GORDON.)

GORDON. Rain's really coming down now, all right.

HELEN. Every afternoon. I remember there was always a storm in the afternoon when I was at my aunt's.

GORDON. Sure does change the feel of things. I love the smell. You ought to go stand on the porch.

HELEN. You really like it out here, don't you?

GORDON. Yes. It makes a lot of difference. It's so quiet.

HELEN. I guess I never think about it all that much.

GORDON. You grew up in places like this, I didn't. I never lived any-where that didn't have suburbs and shopping centers every-where you looked. This is how kids should grow up, in places like this. Where they have plenty of room, playing in the woods, swimming in the river, all that.

HELEN (*changing the subject*). Well, if I don't get this supper started we won't eat till midnight.

GORDON. I told you I'll take you out.

HELEN. I know. But I don't want to go anywhere, not tonight.

> (*Exit* HELEN.
>
> *Rain begins to fall in earnest.*
>
> GORDON *continues to admire the storm.*)

GORDON. God I love the country. Look at that. All across the field, just pouring down. Makes you think of—all kinds of things. Farming. Plants growing. All that stuff. New thoughts. All that stuff. Makes you feel almost like being alive again. Living out here. Not like Sandy Springs. I still can't believe we found this place. (*Laughs softly, calls to* HELEN.) Helen, do you want a drink? I think I'll have one.

> (HELEN *does not respond.*
>
> GORDON *shrugs and pours himself a glass of bourbon, neat.*
>
> *A soft knock sounds.*
>
> GORDON *watches the entrance warily and decides he has not heard any knocking.*
>
> *After a moment the knock sounds again.*
>
> GORDON *answers the door.*
>
> *Enter* ELEANOR, *wet, in worn clothes and shoes.*)

GORDON. Hello.

ELEANOR. I'm real sorry to bother you.

GORDON. Yes?

ELEANOR. I live across the field over there.

GORDON. Yes?

ELEANOR. I'm real sorry. (*Pause.*) Could you . . . could I . . . come in, just for a minute? (*Looks over her shoulder.*) To use the phone.

GORDON. Don't you have a phone at your house?

ELEANOR. No.

GORDON. Oh. (*Pause.*) Sort of wet out there.

ELEANOR. Rain's coming down pretty good, all right.

GORDON. Did you walk all the way across the field, in it?

ELEANOR. I was ... already outside. When the storm started.

> (*The phone should be close to the entry.*
>
> GORDON *hands her the receiver.*)

GORDON. Do you know the number you want to call? The book is right here.

> (GORDON *hands her the book, which should be small, befitting a rural area.*
>
> *He returns to his drink, watching her.*
>
> ELEANOR *looks up the number.*
>
> *She is embarrassed, conscious of her wetness in the pretty house.*)

ELEANOR. I hope I don't mess up your floor.

GORDON. Don't worry about it, it's got a good seal.

> (*She looks at the phone.*
>
> *Suddenly she becomes afraid and freezes.*
>
> GORDON, *in spite of himself, watches.*
>
> *She dials the phone, then after a moment presses down the switch hook and holds it down.*
>
> *She repeats this.*
>
> *She dials again and this time lets the phone ring, though it need not be heard, but she hangs it up soon after.*
>
> *She is agitated, near tears.*)

ELEANOR. It's busy.

GORDON. Would you like to wait? To call again?

ELEANOR. Thank you. I don't guess I should.

GORDON (*showing the slightest sympathy for the first time*). Are you sure? You really can wait.

ELEANOR. Thank you, I ought to go.

> (ELEANOR *turns to go.*
>
> *Enter* HELEN.)

HELEN. I can hear you out here Gordon, have you started talking to yourself? (*Sees* ELEANOR.) Oh. Hello, Eleanor.

ELEANOR. Good evening, ma'am.

HELEN (*glancing at* GORDON). I didn't hear anyone come in.

ELEANOR (*heading to the door*). I come to use the phone. Your husband showed me where it was. And now I ought to get home.

HELEN. You're not going out again. Gordon. Don't tell me you were going to let her out in that storm again.

GORDON. I asked her to wait. But she said she just wanted to use the phone.

> (HELEN *simply watches him for a moment.*)

HELEN. You know perfectly well she doesn't just need to use the phone. She's soaked. Get my robe from the bedroom, please, Gordon. The big one. And bring towels.

> (*They have a moment of silent argument.*
>
> *Exit* GORDON.)

HELEN. You're half-frozen.

ELEANOR. It was a pretty big storm.

HELEN. I wish you . . . had come here sooner.

> (*The women watch each other.*
>
> HELEN *discovers a bruise on* ELEANOR's *face.*
>
> *Enter* GORDON, *with robe and towels.*)

GORDON. This yellow one is it, right?

HELEN. Yes.

> (ELEANOR *removes* HELEN's *hand from the bruise before*
> GORDON *sees it.*)

HELEN. Go clear out the bathroom down here, Gordon, so it's fit for her to go in. There's towels and fur all over the place from when you shampooed the dog.

GORDON. I didn't clean those up yet?

HELEN (*to* ELEANOR). Listen to him, so innocent. (*To* GORDON.) No, you didn't, and you know it. And I told you I wasn't going to do it this time, and I'm not.

GORDON (*exiting*). All right, all right.

HELEN. I've told him to wash the dog outside but he won't listen. He thinks a dog is people. The dog has to take a bath in the bathtub and dry off with my good towels.

ELEANOR. I don't let any dogs in my house.

HELEN. Do you keep dogs?

ELEANOR. My children have two. Mongrels, both of them. Look like wolfs.

>   (*Silence.*
>
>   *By now* ELEANOR *is in the robe, which she admires.*)

HELEN. Your husband was looking for you. Out in the field.

ELEANOR. I didn't see him.

HELEN. He was walking along the edge of the field. On this side. At the beginning of the rain.

>   (ELEANOR *does not respond.*
>
>   HELEN *goes to the window.*)

HELEN. Do you think he's still out there?

ELEANOR. Yes.

HELEN. Even in all this rain?

ELEANOR. He don't care about the rain.

>   (*Enter* GORDON.)

GORDON. All clear, clean and shining.

HELEN. I certainly hope so. (*To* ELEANOR.) Now you just go in there and get yourself straight. Take a bath if you want to. Everything's right there. Through that door to the left. Do you want me to show you?

ELEANOR (*exiting*). No ma'am, I'll be fine.

(*Exit* ELEANOR.

HELEN *follows her almost to the exit.*)

HELEN (*to* ELEANOR). Are you hungry? Would you like some hot soup or a sandwich?

(*No answer.*

HELEN *watches* GORDON *for a moment, then goes to the window.*)

GORDON. You think she knows what to do in there?

HELEN. What do you mean?

GORDON. She may not have ever seen an indoor toilet before. And you got so many knickknacks in there, she may not know how to act.

HELEN. Don't be hateful.

GORDON. I'm just speculating. Don't mind me.

(*Silence.*)

HELEN. I can't believe you didn't tell me when she got here.

GORDON. Well you found out, didn't you?

HELEN. Only because I came out here. You should have come to the kitchen and got me.

GORDON. What for? All she wanted was to use the phone. I let her. We didn't need you out here to play hostess.

HELEN. Gordon, I know just exactly how true that is. Now don't say it again. (*Pause.*) Who did she call?

GORDON. I don't know.

HELEN. Couldn't you hear her talking?

GORDON. She didn't exactly call anybody. She never got an answer. She said the line was busy.

HELEN. And so you decided to send her back out in the rain. With that man out there looking for her.

GORDON. I did not send her back out in the rain. And that man is her husband.

HELEN. Who apparently beat her up and chased her into the woods.

GORDON. You're making too much out of this. You don't know whether he beat her up or not.

HELEN. Did you see her face?

GORDON (*raising his voice just slightly*). Yes I saw it.

HELEN. Keep your voice down. Did you see the bruise on her eye? How do you think it got there?

GORDON. Well, Helen, I guess what matters at this point is how you think it got there. Since you're so obsessed with this whole thing.

HELEN. I'm not obsessed.

GORDON. Yes you are. And you're all emotional about it. And you're not making any sense. You have this woman in our bathroom getting dressed up in your good robe and you have a chicken half cut up rotting in the kitchen and you won't get ten feet away from that goddamn window. God knows what you've got planned for the rest of the evening.

HELEN. Somebody has to help her.

GORDON. No, Helen. No. Nobody has to help her. She has to go home. That's where she belongs. She has to go home to her own family and her own husband, because that's her place and that's where she belongs.

HELEN. Her place?

GORDON. You know what I mean.

HELEN. No, Gordon, I don't know what you mean.

GORDON. Stop twisting my words around. We're not talking about my opinions on women, we're talking about one poor woman who doesn't know any better than to run into the woods in a rainstorm when she has a fight with her husband. She shouldn't be dragging us into her problems by coming over here. That's all I meant. Sympathy doesn't have much to do with it.

HELEN. You can't do that. You can't decide somebody is trash and worthless and throw them out in the rain.

GORDON. That's not what I'm doing.

HELEN. Yes it is.

GORDON. No it's not. Listen to me, Helen. Listen.

HELEN. I won't. Not to this. You can't look at her dress and her house and decide you know everything about her.

GORDON. She's a poor ignorant woman who had too many children too quick and got in way over her head. And there's nothing we can do about that even if we try.

HELEN (*after a moment*). You're wrong.

GORDON. You're not listening to me. (*Pause.*) When are you going to make dinner?

HELEN. I am listening to you.

GORDON. Answer my question.

> (*Silence.*
>
> HELEN *checks the window again.*
>
> Enter ELEANOR *in the robe.*
>
> She hesitates, feeling the awkwardness.*)

HELEN. It's all right. Come on in. You all dry now?

ELEANOR. Yes ma'am. I left my clothes in the bathroom. I didn't know what else to do, they're wringing wet.

HELEN. Don't you worry about that, I'll take care of it. I'll pop them in the wash. You feel better?

ELEANOR. I sure do.

HELEN. Are you hungry yet? My husband is about to worry me to death to get him something to eat.

ELEANOR. No ma'am, I couldn't eat anything. But don't let me get in your way, I know it's suppertime.

HELEN. You're not in anybody's way. (*Prepares to exit; speaks to* GORDON.) Well, let me go put up that chicken and make you a sandwich. I don't feel like eating either and there's no use frying a whole chicken for one person. Do you think so?

GORDON. Oh of course not. (*Pause.*)

HELEN (*to* Eleanor). You sit down and rest. I'll be back in a minute. And don't pay any attention to anything my husband tells you, he won't bite. You like coffee?

ELEANOR. Yes ma'am.

HELEN. I'll bring you a cup.

> (*Exit* HELEN.
>
> GORDON *follows her to see where she is going.*
> *Once she is out of sight, he turns and goes to the window,*
> *considering* ELEANOR.)

GORDON. So you feel better?

ELEANOR. Yes sir.

GORDON. I hope you didn't think I was trying to get rid of you.

ELEANOR. Oh, no sir.

GORDON. I didn't really know what you wanted.

ELEANOR. That's all right.

GORDON. I'm very protective of my wife.

ELEANOR. Yes sir.

GORDON. My wife is very tender hearted.

ELEANOR. She's a real nice lady. (*Pause.*) I won't stay long, Mr. Hammond.

GORDON. You're perfectly welcome. (*Pause.*) Helen thinks you're having a fight with your husband.

(ELEANOR *does not know how to respond.*)

GORDON. You don't have to be ashamed of it. People have fights.

ELEANOR. Yes sir.

GORDON. My wife and I had a little bit of an argument tonight.

ELEANOR. Yes sir.

GORDON. It might be that you need to get some professional help. Some type of counseling.

ELEANOR. My husband don't like to talk a whole lot. Especially to preachers and people like that.

GORDON. I'm sure he wants to do what's good for you. And for his children. A father would want to do the best thing for his children and a husband would want to do the best thing for his wife. Don't you think that's true? I mean, laying aside the fact that you're having a fight with him. Don't you think he wants to do what's best? In the long run?

ELEANOR. He's real mad right now.

GORDON. But when he calms down. You can talk to him then.

ELEANOR. Talking don't work with Jake.

GORDON. You're pretty upset yourself right now, aren't you? I expect you're selling him a little short. I expect he feels pretty bad about the whole argument right now. And you do too.

ELEANOR. I didn't do anything. And he's not sorry.

GORDON. Be fair now. (*Pause;* ELEANOR *does not respond.*) He must be a good man or you wouldn't have married him. You must love him. Or you wouldn't have married him.

ELEANOR. Men change when they get married.

GORDON. What do you mean?

ELEANOR. They get spiteful.

GORDON. Well, I got married and I didn't get spiteful.

(ELEANOR *simply looks at him.*

As GORDON *speaks, he freshens his bourbon.*)

GORDON. The fact is you're mad with him and you're not thinking straight right now. When you're calmer you'll see I'm right.

(*Enter* HELEN, *with a tray of sandwiches and coffee.*)

HELEN. I thought you were just having one drink.

GORDON. I'm just having one more.

HELEN. Well I hope so. Because if you're hung over and grouchy when I wake you up tomorrow, I'm going to let you lay there. Mark my words.

GORDON. Yes dear.

HELEN (*to* ELEANOR). He can't wake up by himself. Not since I quit my job. When we lived in Atlanta and I had to get up first, the alarm clock could wake him up just fine but now he has two alarm clocks that go off like firecrackers and he won't even turn over. I have to get up first and make his coffee, and then I have to talk real sweet in his ear before he'll even open his eyes.

GORDON. Now that's not fair. I have to get up a whole lot earlier than I did when we lived in town.

HELEN. The way things turned out, so do I. (*To* ELEANOR). I made little sandwiches for you and me. You like cucumber?

ELEANOR. Oh, yes ma'am. I got a garden full of it.

HELEN. I never could get a thing to grow. All my flowers just die in the pot. (*Setting down the tray; to* GORDON.) I fried you a little steak on a bun, Gordon. Like you like, with the onions.

GORDON. I was about to say, I hope you don't expect me to eat any cucumber sandwich.

HELEN. Oh, I know better than that. If it don't have meat in it, it's not food.

(*Each eats and drinks.*

ELEANOR *eats delicately, distracted, as if she does not
taste the sandwich.*

GORDON *eats his steak with gusto.*

HELEN *does not eat but sips coffee by the window, looking out.*)

GORDON. We've been having a nice talk out here, Helen. I've been
telling Eleanor about counseling and things like that.

HELEN. Counseling?

GORDON. For married people.

HELEN. I'm sure Eleanor knows about those things.

GORDON. It's something to think about.

HELEN. I never could stand counselors and psychiatrists and people like that. I used to work with them and I never could stand
the way they talked.

ELEANOR. You don't have a job anymore?

HELEN. No, I don't. I quit working not long ago. (*Pause.*) Do you
think your children are all right?

ELEANOR. My oldest girl is looking out for the little ones. She
fusses at them just like I do.

HELEN. Is that the little brown-haired girl? She's pretty as a button.

ELEANOR. She's seven. She's real smart in school.

GORDON. How many children do you have?

ELEANOR. Five.

GORDON. How do you keep them all straight? If it was me, I would
get them mixed up. Call them the wrong names.

HELEN. Don't be ridiculous, Gordon. Five is not that many.

ELEANOR. It's plenty for me. I hope I don't have any more.

HELEN. Gordon and I would be glad to have just one. We've been
trying. But we haven't had much luck so far.

GORDON. Hush.

ELEANOR. With my husband, I don't even have to try.

HELEN (*to* GORDON). It's not bad luck to talk about it. (*Looking out the window.*) I see him again. He's still out there.

ELEANOR. Is he?

HELEN. Yes. Down by that piece of fence. (*Pause.*) Oh Lord. It looks like he's coming up here.

GORDON. Christ! Are you sure?

HELEN (*still looking out into the storm; to* ELEANOR). Go back into the kitchen. I'll be back there in a minute. (*To* GORDON.) You tell him you haven't seen anything at all.

(*Exit* ELEANOR.)

GORDON. You beat everything.

HELEN. Please do this. Please.

GORDON. Fine. I will get him out of here without a scene. But you listen. When her clothes are dry she gets out of here too. That minute. And then you and I are going to have a long talk.

HELEN. You can lecture me till you're blue in the face once you get rid of that man.

(*A shadow crosses one of the windows.*

A knock sounds at the door.)

GORDON. What the hell is his name?

HELEN (*exiting*). Jake. That's what she said.

(*Knock sounds again.*

GORDON *answers the door.*

Enter JAKE, *carrying a rain poncho and cap.*

He is relatively dry.)

JAKE. Good e'enin.

GORDON. Good evening. Looks like you picked a nice night for a walk. Is there something I can do for you?

JAKE. Sure is. You reckon I could come in for a minute?

GORDON. Please. Be my guest.

JAKE. Could I trouble you for an old towel or a rag to dry my shoes? I sure would hate to track your floors.

GORDON. No trouble at all. I'll be right back.

> (*Exit* GORDON.
>
> JAKE *inspects the room quickly.*
>
> *He goes to the tray and lifts the glass and the two coffee cups, one at a time, then seats himself.*
>
> *Enter* GORDON.)

GORDON. Pretty good storm out there.

JAKE. It'll do. (*Offering his hand congenially.*) You prob'ly don't know me, sir, but I'm your neighbor in that house over yonder cross the field, and my name is Jake Rollins, and I was wondering if you had seen my wife. She run off. Just before suppertime.

> (JAKE *takes the towel after they have shaken hands and begins to dry his shoes.*)

GORDON. She ran off, you said?

JAKE. Yes sir. (*Sighs.*) We had a little fight. It was really a big mix-up, you know? And my wife, she run off in the woods. And she's still there I guess. Me and the children is worried sick.

GORDON. Sounds like you've had yourself quite an evening.

JAKE. It can get right wild over there. (*Looks around the room.*) So she didn't come over here.

GORDON. No. No, it's just my wife and me here. And my wife's not feeling too good.

JAKE. I'm sorry to hear that, sir. I hope it's nothing serious.

GORDON. She's lying down with a headache.

JAKE (*looking around the house*). This a pretty nice house. You must do good for yourself. You work in Atlanta?

GORDON. Yes. I'm an accountant. For a big company.

JAKE. That's a pretty good drive.

GORDON. Some days I don't have to go in. I'm a partner now. That's why we bought this house.

JAKE. That's a good situation. (*Pause.*) You grow up in Atlanta?

GORDON. Vinings.

JAKE. Where's that?

GORDON (*shrugs*). Atlanta, basically.

JAKE. Like a suburb?

GORDON. Sort of. But it's a pretty old town. My grandfather moved there from Alabama.

JAKE. I got an uncle from Alabama. He don't like it.

GORDON. My wife was born somewhere around here. But her family moved to Sandy Springs when she was pretty young.

JAKE. Where is that?

GORDON. Atlanta.

JAKE. You built this place? (*Pause.*) No, that's right, it was them other people built it, I forget the name.

GORDON. McKinley. They sold it to us. We saw it in an ad. Just what we wanted. We were very lucky.

JAKE. You bet you were. You got a swimming pool?

GORDON. No. No we don't have anything like that yet. (*Pause.*) But my wife was able to quit her job. When I got promoted. I had to talk her into it but she finally agreed. We plan to raise a family. Soon. (*Pause.*) You and your family moved in that house a little while ago.

JAKE. Yeah. It ain't nothing but a shack.

GORDON. Oh.

JAKE. My wife, she's always talking about getting us a trailer. You can buy you a pretty nice trailer. (*Pause.*) I wouldn't hardly know how to act in a house like this.

GORDON. I sure hate to picture your wife out in this storm. You been looking for her long?

JAKE. She run off right before the storm come up. I had to get my poncho. But I been all down the river. She likes to walk around there. She's moody-like, you know.

GORDON. Maybe she found some shelter and is waiting for the rain to stop.

JAKE. You know, I didn't even think about that. I bet she crawled up under that bridge. What do you want to bet?

GORDON. Now that would make sense, wouldn't it?

JAKE. Sure would. (*Pause.*) Women are so excitable. You know it? The least little thing can just set them right off.

GORDON (*laughing*). I sure do know that.

JAKE. And then you might as well forget it. When a woman gets something in her mind she'll worry it to death, you know it? It's no use to try to talk to her. She can't listen to sense.

GORDON. I guess every husband feels like that sometimes.

JAKE. You can't make sense to the women and the women can't make sense to you.

GORDON. It makes you wonder if they think the same way we do.

JAKE. You know, I've had that same thought. I can see you got a good understanding of women.

GORDON. I don't know about that.

JAKE (*standing*). So you're sure you haven't seen my wife? Little skinny woman. She ain't got much ass, to tell you the truth. That's half of her problem. (*Laughs.*)

GORDON (*laughing with him*). No. No, I haven't seen nobody like that tonight.

JAKE. Not even walking across your yard or nothing.

GORDON. No. Sorry.

JAKE. Well, then, let me get down to that bridge and see if I can find my baby. If you see her, you tell her I'm looking for her. You hear?

GORDON (*nodding*). I sure do sympathize with you.

JAKE. Oh, I'll find her sooner or later. And I'll get her all calmed down again. I always do. (*Pause.*) You and your wife have a good night, hear?

GORDON. We'll try. I know one thing, I'm not going outdoors in this mess.

JAKE. I can't blame you. I wouldn't either if it won't for my baby.

(*Exit* JAKE.

This time, however, his shadow does not cross the window.

Enter HELEN, *tiptoeing.*)

HELEN. Is he gone?

GORDON. Yes.

HELEN. He sure stayed a long time.

GORDON. Not that long. We were talking.

HELEN. I'm surprised you could find anything to talk about.

GORDON. Helen, I couldn't throw him out the second he got here.

HELEN (*almost an aside*). You could when it was her.

(*Silence.*)

GORDON. I don't think he believed me. He asked me if I had seen her three or four times.

HELEN. You didn't tell him, did you?

GORDON. No. I was a good boy, I did what you told me to do. (*Pause.*) He told me about the fight. It didn't sound like much.

HELEN. What did he say?

(*Enter* ELEANOR *unseen by* GORDON.)

GORDON. He said the fight was just a mix-up. But he acted like he didn't want to talk about it. He said he didn't know why she ran off, she just did. And he tried to find her because he's worried about her.

ELEANOR. That's not what happened. He twists everything around. He come home drunk, is what happened.

(HELEN *crosses to the window.*)

HELEN. I don't see him. (*To* ELEANOR.) Do you think he went home?

GORDON. He said he was going down to the bridge. To see if she was under it, keeping dry.

ELEANOR. He knows I wouldn't get under that bridge, because of snakes.

GORDON. All I know is what he told me.

ELEANOR. He hasn't gone anywhere. He's still outside. He knows I'm in here.

HELEN. Tell us what happened, Eleanor. When he came home.

ELEANOR (*afraid to talk*). He got off work early, like he does on payday. That's today. He had a bag with him and I knew what it was. And he was already drinking. And we had a fight while I was fixing supper and he hit me some and I run out of the house.

HELEN. He made that bruise on your face.

ELEANOR. Yes ma'am. (*Pause.*) But that was from last night.

HELEN. We're calling the sheriff. Right now.

GORDON. Helen—

ELEANOR. It won't do any good.

HELEN. Of course it will, if you press charges. They'll put him in jail.

ELEANOR. They took him off last night. To the motel, not to jail. They buy gas at the filling station where he works, so they hate to lock him up. He come right back home.

HELEN. But he can't beat you up like that. There's got to be something you can do about it.

ELEANOR. I never been able to before.

> (*Lights go suddenly to black.*
>
> *Light from outside floods through the windows.*)

GORDON. Hell. I didn't hear any thunder.

HELEN. The light in the yard is still on.

> (*A sound is heard, like someone stumbling over cans.*
>
> *A dog barks.*)

GORDON. Christ, there goes Henry.

HELEN. But I shut him up in the utility room when the storm
started.

GORDON. Well it sure sounds like he got out. (*Looks outside.*) Why
would the lights go out because it's raining? And the light in
the yard burning just as pretty as you please.

ELEANOR. It's Jake.

GORDON. What do you mean?

ELEANOR. Jake did this. Shut off the power.

GORDON (*understanding*). He went in the utility room. That's how
the dog got out.

HELEN. He did this on purpose?

ELEANOR. Yes ma'am.

HELEN. But why would he?

> (JAKE's *shadow crosses slowly to the center of one of the*
> *windows.*
>
> *He is clearly backlit.*
>
> *Those inside freeze.*)

GORDON. All right. This has gone far enough.

HELEN (*softly*). Keep your voice down.

GORDON. She's going home. Now.

HELEN. No she is not. She is coming with me to the back of the
house and you're going to tell him one more time she's not

here. And then we're going to call the sheriff and have him arrested for trespassing.

> (JAKE *saunters out of sight toward the front door.*
> *Exit* HELEN *and* ELEANOR.
> GORDON *is motionless until the knock on the door.*
> *He answers the door after the second knock.*
> *Enter* JAKE, *poncho dripping.*
> *His manner is different this time, no longer as polite.*)

JAKE. I sure am sorry to bother you twice in one evening like this.
But did you see that bolt of lightning struck your garage? Just
a minute ago, at the back?

GORDON. We didn't notice any lightning.

JAKE. Well I sure don't know how you missed it. I was halfway to
the bridge and come back to see if anything was wrong. Looks
like nothing caught fire.

GORDON. It was kind of you to check.

JAKE. Lights are out, huh?

GORDON. Sure looks that way.

JAKE. Maybe it just tripped the breaker. You got breakers? Or fuses?

GORDON. Breakers. I guess I'll go check in a minute.

JAKE. You want some company?

GORDON. No. I'll be all right by myself.

JAKE. You sure?

GORDON. Yes. I wouldn't want to keep you.

JAKE (*laughing*). Sure was stupid of them McKinleys to put the
breaker box in the garage. You know it? (*Pause.*) I found my
wife.

GORDON. Was she under the bridge?

JAKE. Oh no, I never got that far. (*Pause.*) Where did your wife go?
I thought I heard her. When I was walking up on the porch.

GORDON. She went back to bed. She just came out to see what happened to the lights.

JAKE. What about that other woman that was with her?

GORDON. What other woman?

JAKE. Come on now. Don't play stupid like some shit-ass.

GORDON. There's no one here except me and my wife.

JAKE. Oh I know who's here, all right. Where is she?

GORDON. I already told you.

JAKE. You scared to admit it? You scared I'm going to come after you or something?

　　　(*Silence.*)

GORDON. She's here. But she'll come out when she wants to. And not before.

JAKE. Don't talk shit to me, mister.

GORDON. I think it's time you left.

JAKE. I'll tell you when I'm ready to leave.

GORDON. Get out of my house before I have you arrested for trespassing.

JAKE. Baby I been arrested before, it don't hold any fear for me. Now you let me tell you something. Shut your mouth and listen to me. Now you tell that bitch that she's got fifteen minutes to drag her puny ass back to the house. And if she don't I'm coming back here for her. Now you tell her that. And you'll be sorry if I do. And from now on if my wife knocks on your door, you tell her to get back home. Because if you don't, you're going to get what's good for you. You listening to me?

GORDON. You can't talk to me like that in my own house.

JAKE. And what the fuck are you going to do about it? Shit-head.

　　　(JAKE *returns to door, which should still be open.*)

JAKE. Now I'm leaving, just like you asked me to. Because I don't want to fight you and if I stay I'm going to bust the shit out of you. But you tell my wife. Fifteen minutes. Or by God I'll make her wish she'd done what I said. And you too.

> (*Exit* JAKE.
>
> GORDON *watches from the doorway.*
>
> *After a moment he closes the door.*
>
> *Enter* HELEN.)

HELEN. Is he gone?

GORDON. Did you hear him?

HELEN. Yes.

GORDON. I felt like I had to tell him.

HELEN. I know.

GORDON. He's not going to talk to me like that.

HELEN. Calm down.

GORDON. Where is she?

HELEN. In the corner room. She's lying down.

GORDON. I can see why she doesn't go home.

HELEN. We can't send her back there.

GORDON. Well what do you want to do?

HELEN. I don' know.

GORDON (*moving to the window*). You better figure it out pretty quick. Because he's still out there in the yard. Watching every move we make.

> (*Blackout.*)

ACT 2

The storm has diminished but continues.

Enter HELEN, *with a tray of candles.*

She lights candles and sets them in various parts of the stage.

Enter GORDON, *after* HELEN *has been onstage long enough to light three candles.*

From his behavior it should be clear he is hiding something.

He stops to watch HELEN.

GORDON. What are you doing?

HELEN. Getting us some light.

GORDON. I'm going outside to turn on the breakers right now.

HELEN. I don't think you should do that.

GORDON. Why not?

HELEN. I don't think you should go out there where he is. You don't have to.

(*Silence.*)

GORDON. Do you think I'm afraid of him?

HELEN. That's not what I said. I said there's no need for you to go out there, that's all.

GORDON. Well, what do you want me to do, sit here in the dark?

HELEN. No. That's why I'm lighting candles.

GORDON. You do think I'm afraid. I knew it.

HELEN. Gordon, don't be silly.

GORDON. What do you think is going to happen if we sit here in a room full of candles? Do you think he's going to wait outside politely while we try to talk his wife into going home with him?

HELEN. I think we should call the sheriff.

GORDON. That will be a big help.

HELEN. You could at least call him and ask if there's anything he can do.

GORDON. Helen, you heard what that woman said.

HELEN. That woman's name is Eleanor.

GORDON. Fine. You heard what Eleanor said. The sheriff and the deputies are this man's friends.

HELEN. So what are you going to do?

GORDON. I'm going to talk to him. I'm going to tell him he can't expect his wife to go home till he calms down.

HELEN. Gordon, that man is not going to listen to a little pep talk and then head home just like that.

GORDON. I'm going to make him listen.

(*Silence.*)

HELEN. We're perfectly safe in here, Gordon. He won't bother us as long as we stay inside.

GORDON. You don't know that.

HELEN. What could he do? All we have to do is lock the doors.

GORDON. He already broke in the utility room and turned off the power. If he says he's coming back inside, he probably is.

HELEN. If you really think that, you have to call the sheriff.

GORDON. Jake hasn't done anything wrong as far as the sheriff is concerned. He came to our house and asked if we had seen his wife.

HELEN. But he turned out the power. Like you said.

GORDON. We're in the middle of a thunderstorm, Helen.

(*Silence.*)

HELEN. I don't want you to go.

GORDON. It's the only thing I know to do. Unless you really want him to come in here and get his wife.

HELEN. No.

GORDON. There's nothing to be afraid of.

HELEN. That's not what she says.

GORDON. I can take care of myself.

HELEN. Well what are you going to do if you go outside? Have a fight with him?

(GORDON *has been concealing a handgun and a box of ammunition all this time. They may be on his person, or he may hide them in the room when he comes onstage.*

If the latter option is chosen, the objects must he hidden in such a way that the audience recognizes the object as a gun no earlier than this moment.

GORDON *now reveals the gun.*

HELEN *simply watches it.)*

HELEN. God help us. When did you get that?

GORDON. When we moved out here.

HELEN. Why?

GORDON. For protection.

HELEN. And you didn't tell me?

GORDON. I knew you would be upset. But I felt like I had to have it.

HELEN. Where do you keep it?

GORDON. With my things.

HELEN. Where?

GORDON. I'm not going to tell you.

HELEN. Oh yes you will. If there's going to be a gun in my house I'm going to know where it is.

GORDON. And then the first time I turn my back you'll throw it in the river.

HELEN. I will certainly think about it.

GORDON. See?

HELEN. Gordon Hammond, you have no right to bring a gun into this house and keep it secret from me.

GORDON. If I told you about it we would only have had another fight.

HELEN. What has happened to you?

GORDON. Helen, we are in the middle of nowhere out here. We'd be fools to sit in this house with nothing but a butter knife for protection.

HELEN. I don't want to be protected that way.

GORDON. Well, Helen, you're not making sense.

(*Silence.*)

HELEN. What are you going to do with it now that you've got it?

GORDON. Put bullets in it. Right now.

HELEN. You're not really going to shoot anybody.

GORDON. I hope not. But I do not intend to let that cracker get back in my house.

(HELEN *continues with the candles.*
She is agitated.)

GORDON. How long has it been?

HELEN. About five minutes.

GORDON. She lying down?

HELEN. I expect so. If she could get him off her mind she could probably sleep. She's exhausted. They fought all last night, from the sound of it.

GORDON. Did you get her to tell you about it?

HELEN. Some. She doesn't like to talk.

GORDON. You probably ought to get her up.

HELEN. Let her lie there for a little while longer.

GORDON. If he comes back here, she's going to want to be where she can run.

HELEN (*from the window*). He's not at the tree anymore.

(GORDON *joins her.*)

GORDON. Where is he? Do you see him?

HELEN. No. But you can't see much. (*Moves to the other window; after a moment.*) He's over here now. By the mailbox.

(GORDON *joins her.*
He blows out the candles nearest the windows.)

HELEN. They look so pretty.

GORDON. He can see inside. With these candles burning. He can see every move we make.

> (*After a moment,* HELEN *blows out one candle, then stops.*
>
> *She is watching* GORDON.)

HELEN. Would you like a cup of coffee?

GORDON. Yes, that would be nice. (*Pause.*) How long's it been?

HELEN. Time's up by now.

GORDON. He's not moving.

HELEN. Maybe he's not wearing a watch.

> (*Exit* HELEN, *to get coffee.*)

GORDON (*studying something more closely*). He's got my dog. He's got my dog with him. (*He calls the dog without raising his voice.*) Henry. Henry! Get away from him, boy. Get away from him. Damnit, dog, get away from him. Stupid dog.

> (*Enter* HELEN, *as* GORDON *speaks.*)

HELEN. What's wrong?

GORDON. The damn dog is out there with him.

HELEN. Henry? What is he doing?

GORDON. Standing there. Nuzzling up to that son of a bitch. I ought to kill him. Both of them.

HELEN. Have you ever even fired that gun?

GORDON. I have taken it to the firing range twice, I will have you know.

HELEN. Twice. And now you are talking about shooting a dog. And a neighbor.

GORDON. He is not a neighbor. He is some trash living in a shack across a cornfield. He is a man in our front yard who does not think well of us, Helen; now will you please think about that for a minute? He is on our property. He is walking around our land like he owns every inch of it. He may try to hurt you if he comes in here again, and he will certainly try to hurt his wife. These are the things somebody has to think about.

(*Enter* ELEANOR.

Seeing the candles, she hangs back in shadow.)

ELEANOR. Where is he?

HELEN. Now what are you doing up here? You know I told you to stay in the back of the house.

ELEANOR. I can't get any rest. Where is he?

GORDON. At the end of the cleared part of our property. Near the mailbox. He's got my dog with him.

(ELEANOR *tries to approach the window but is afraid to cross in front of the candles.*)

ELEANOR. He can see inside with these.

HELEN. Does that worry you?

ELEANOR. Yes ma'am.

HELEN. Please stop calling me "ma'am."

(HELEN *blows out any candles that are in* ELEANOR'*s path but does not blow out all of them.*)

HELEN. Do you think he's coming back? It's past fifteen minutes by now.

ELEANOR. He'll come when he gets ready.

(ELEANOR *goes to the window, looks outside.*

She should show no fear of the gun but should notice it.)

ELEANOR. Are you going to use that on my husband?

GORDON. I don't plan on shooting anybody unless violence occurs.

(*Gestures out the window with the gun.*) See him, over there?

ELEANOR. See what?

GORDON. Your husband.

ELEANOR. That doesn't look like Jake.

GORDON. Of course it's Jake. He's wearing a poncho. Who else would it be?

ELEANOR. It's not him. It's not anybody. See?

GORDON. I know what I see.

ELEANOR. He hung his poncho and his rain hat on a stick.

GORDON. I watched him walk over there. And he's been standing there ever since.

ELEANOR. Jake would never let a dog sniff at him like that.

> (*Lights come on suddenly, just as they were in the first*
> *act when the power went off.*
>
> ELEANOR *jumps back from the window.*)

GORDON. That son of a bitch.

HELEN. Come away from the window.

GORDON. He tricked me. The son of a bitch. He's in the garage.

> (GORDON *moves briefly toward the door, then turns off*
> *the lights, either by switching off any individual*
> *lamps onstage or by turning off an overhead light*
> *switch.*)

ELEANOR. He's not in the garage anymore.

GORDON. Where is he?

ELEANOR. In the yard.

GORDON. In the rain? Without a poncho?

ELEANOR. He don't care about the rain. Besides, listen. It's slacked off.

> (*They listen to the storm, which has lessened consider-*
> *ably in force.*)

HELEN. Come away from the window, Gordon.

GORDON. He can't see me.

HELEN. Yes he can. Please.

GORDON (*doing as she asks*). I can take care of myself.

HELEN. You don't need to take care of yourself, you need to call the sheriff.

GORDON. I've told you I am not calling anybody.

ELEANOR. Sheriff's not any help anyway.

HELEN. Both of you keep saying that. But he certainly will help. If you explain the whole situation to him. He'll arrest your husband for trespassing on our property.

ELEANOR. Time the sheriff pulls in the driveway, Jake will be long gone from your yard.

HELEN. Well they can still arrest him for doing it. For being on it in the first place. For turning off the fuses.

GORDON. Breakers. We have breakers.

HELEN. All right then, for turning off the. The damn breakers. Whatever. The sheriff will be able to do something about that.

GORDON (*attempting to embrace her*). Calm down, Helen. I'm right here.

HELEN (*pulling away from him*). Don't. Just don't.

GORDON. What's wrong with you?

HELEN. Don't talk to me like I don't have good sense.

(*Silence.*)

ELEANOR. I wish you would shoot him.

GORDON. You sound serious.

ELEANOR. Sometimes I think I could do it myself.

GORDON. Have you ever used a gun before?

ELEANOR. My little boy has a BB gun.

GORDON. Oh well. (*Lifting the gun.*) That's nothing like this.

(*Silence.*

GORDON *moves from window to window, finally to the door.*)

HELEN. What are you doing?

GORDON. Just looking.

HELEN. But he can see you.

GORDON. Would you stop being ridiculous? I'm not afraid. (*Looking out.*) I'll probably go out there soon.

HELEN. Come away from the door. Close it.

GORDON. You're not listening to me. I think what I have to do is go out there. Talk some sense to him.

HELEN. You think he's going to listen to you talk sense with a gun in your hand?

GORDON. I'll put it in my pocket. My raincoat. Right in the pocket.

HELEN. You have lost your mind. If you go out there I will call the sheriff myself.

GORDON. You'll do no such thing.

HELEN. She is not going home, Gordon.

GORDON. I didn't say a word about that. Where is my raincoat?

HELEN. In the closet. Where it always is, unless it walks around when I'm not looking.

GORDON. Get it for me, would you?

> (GORDON *should be looking out the door when he says*
> *this.*
>
> HELEN *simply watches him for a moment; exit* HELEN.)

ELEANOR. Tell him I'll come on home.

GORDON. I don't think I should do that.

ELEANOR. Yes you do.

GORDON. What I was going to tell him was, I don't think you should go home till he calms down.

ELEANOR. He won't calm down if I stay here.

> (*Silence.*)

GORDON. Are you sure?

ELEANOR. Yes sir.

GORDON. You're welcome to stay.

ELEANOR. No. I'm not.

GORDON. I'll tell him you'll be home in half an hour. Is that enough time?

ELEANOR. Yes sir, that's fine.

GORDON. You think that will calm him down?

ELEANOR. It might.

(*Silence.*)

GORDON. I'm sorry. I don't know what else to do.

ELEANOR. Yes sir. (*Pause.*) I don't think you should tell your wife. When the half hour is up, I'll just go.

GORDON (*laughing softly*). She wouldn't let you do it, would she?

(*Enter* HELEN, *with raincoat.*)

HELEN. Wouldn't let her do what?

GORDON (*taking the raincoat*). We were just talking about Eleanor's little girl.

HELEN. She's such a pretty thing. (*As* GORDON *puts on the raincoat.*) Are you sure you ought to do this?

GORDON. Yes. I'll be fine.

(*Exit* GORDON, *after putting the gun in his pocket.*
ELEANOR *remains in place, listening to the whole world.*
HELEN *goes to the windows, roams the stage as the
following dialogue occurs.*)

ELEANOR. I ought to get my dress and go. My children are probably scared to death.

HELEN. Let Gordon talk to him. Maybe it will work, maybe it will calm him down.

(*Silence.*)

HELEN. Did you mean what you said? About shooting him?

ELEANOR. I don't know.

HELEN. You must think about it. Sometimes.

ELEANOR. Yes ma'am. I do.

HELEN. Please don't call me "ma'am." Call me Helen.

ELEANOR. It's not the way I was raised.

(*Silence.*)

HELEN. You must love him. To stay with him like this.

(ELEANOR *laughs very softly.*)

HELEN. Maybe you don't.

ELEANOR. I'm sorry. It's just funny.

HELEN. I can't imagine.

ELEANOR. I never should have come in here.

HELEN. What would you have done?

ELEANOR. Usually I just stay outside.

HELEN. All night?

ELEANOR. It depends. Sometimes he'll go on to sleep and I can get back in the house. But sometimes he don't sleep at all. It's like there's something on his mind that worries at him till he can't rest.

HELEN. Does he usually hunt for you, like tonight?

ELEANOR. No ma'am. (*Pause.*) He's real mad tonight.

HELEN. So you don't think he'll leave you alone. Even if you do go home.

ELEANOR. I don't know what he'll do.

HELEN. Isn't there something else you can do? I hate to think of you over there and this all happening again.

ELEANOR. Yes ma'am. I know you do.

(*Silence.*

ELEANOR *moves cautiously around the room in the
quiet, occasionally glancing out the windows.
Her purpose is to admire the objects in the room and the
house itself, though she is afraid to touch anything.*)

HELEN. What are you looking at?

ELEANOR. Just your house. I like it. Even in the dark.

HELEN. Thank you. I think I like it too.

ELEANOR. It must be something, living in a great big place like Atlanta.

HELEN. It's a nice city. In a lot of ways.

ELEANOR. I used to wish we would move there. Me and Jake and the younguns. I thought maybe Jake would make more money in a big place like that. But Jake, he says there's too many blacks.

HELEN. I guess a lot of people must feel like that. Seems like all the white people are moving north.

ELEANOR. Why did you folks move way out here?

HELEN. I don't know. I used to. But I'm not sure anymore. (*Pause.*) We don't have any children. I told you that already, didn't I?

ELEANOR. Yes ma'am.

HELEN. We've been married ten years. That's a long time, for just two people. And last year Gordon got a big promotion and he was making enough that I didn't need to work. (*Pause.*) So we started talking about it. And we decided if we were ever going to have children, we needed to do it soon. And then we found this house. And Gordon fell in love with it. And so we bought this place and I quit my job. And now I'm trying to get pregnant.

ELEANOR. But you're not.

HELEN. No. (*Pause.*) We've been working at it.

ELEANOR. I'm sorry.

HELEN. Oh, it'll be fine. I'm healthy enough to have a baby, the doctor said so. (*Pause.*) But it's been a long year. Way out here. Funny how it worked out. Gordon was the one who wanted to move out here so bad. But I'm the one who's here all the time.

(*Silence.*

They listen.

The storm has lessened.)

ELEANOR. Storm's breaking.

HELEN. Yes. Smell. (*She smiles.*) I had an aunt who lived near here. Not that close, about an hour away. Naugaton. I stayed on her farm sometimes. And it would always rain in the afternoon. I thought it was so peaceful, the rain and the wind and the trees. Every day. They had a pretty farm. It's not there anymore, they sold it to somebody.

ELEANOR. Did you grow up in Atlanta?

HELEN. Yes. Sandy Springs. We moved there when I was little, before they built all over it. I hate going back there now. (*Pause.*) Do you see anything out there?

ELEANOR. No ma'am.

(*Silence.*)

HELEN. Why did you marry your husband?

(*Silence.*)

ELEANOR. He was a sweet boy, Mrs. Hammond. When I first knew him. I was at a fair with my friend Ginny and he was winning this dart game, and I was watching him. Because I didn't know how to throw anything and he was real good at it. And he saw I was watching. And he liked it. And we kind of fell into each other. I thought it was a good thing then, to have such a wild feeling for somebody. I thought it was what was supposed to happen. To get me away from my papa and my brothers. But now I don't know, I wish the feeling wasn't so wild, or Jake wasn't so wild, or something.

(*Gunshot is heard.*)

HELEN. Dear God.

(ELEANOR *withdraws to shadow.*

HELEN *stands motionless for a moment.*

She takes a deep breath and goes to the phone.

She fumbles with the phone book in the dark, takes it to

a lamp or to the overhead light switch.)

HELEN. I have to turn on the light.

(ELEANOR *flattens herself in the corner between the*

windows.)

ELEANOR. Yes ma'am. I'm ready.

HELEN. What do I look up?

ELEANOR. The sheriff. John Anderson. But he won't be at the office. And he won't be at home either, his wife left him and he stays out half the night. You ought to call the deputy, his name is Mike McAlister. Right at the beginning of M.

HELEN. In Potter's Lake?

ELEANOR. No ma'am. Somersville. It's where the courthouse is and it's where the deputy lives. But the sheriff lives in Potter's Lake.

HELEN. Yes I know, and his wife left him.

ELEANOR. For a black man. She was a teacher.

HELEN (*turning on light, fumbling quickly through the book*). Dear God, I'm scared to death. This is the hardest phone book to use, there's so many towns. There ought to be one list.

ELEANOR. Nobody would like that.

(HELEN *finds the town and then the number hurriedly.*

She dials the number.

The phone rings many times before she gets an answer.)

HELEN. Does the deputy stay out all night too—(*Into the receiver.*) Hello. Hello. Is this—(*Pause.*) Oh yes. Well is your husband there? This is Helen Hammond. (*Pause.*) Helen Hammond. (*Pause.*) Well, I don't know you either. I've never met you. I live on River Road. (*Pause.*) Yes, that's right. From Atlanta. Is your husband there? (*Pause.*) Oh. Well yes. Have him call me. Yes ma'am. 523-7432. Yes ma'am. That's right. Please. I have a problem around my house. (*Hangs up, looks at the phone.*) He's on a call. (*Pause.*) Why didn't I just tell her there was a gunshot?

> (ELEANOR, *hearing something, motions for silence.*
> JAKE *crosses slowly in front of the windows, bare-handed, shirtless, his shadow falling against the sheers.*
> HELEN *silently flattens herself against the wall, kneeling.*
> ELEANOR *freezes.*
> JAKE *stands in front of one of the windows, peers inside.*
> *After a good look, he moves on, rattles the door but does not attempt to come inside.*
> HELEN *looks to see if it is locked.*
> ELEANOR *peers out the window.*)

ELEANOR. He's gone off the porch.

HELEN. But where's Gordon? (*She moves to a window.*) Do you see him?

ELEANOR. No ma'am.

HELEN. I should call her back. The deputy's wife. I should let her know this is important.

ELEANOR. Could you please get me my dress?

HELEN. Oh heavens. Yes. Yes. I'm sorry.

> (*Exit* HELEN, *in some confusion.*
> *Enter* HELEN, *with dress.*
> ELEANOR *changes clothes.*)

ELEANOR. Maybe you ought to check the doors.

HELEN. Ought to what?

ELEANOR. Check the doors. See if they're locked. (*Listening.*) He's close. Jake is.

> (*Tapping is heard backstage, like a fist on the siding of a house.*)

HELEN. I don't think I locked the back door.

> (*The tapping continues.*
>
> HELEN *moves toward the back of the house but becomes afraid.*)

HELEN. Dear God. How can you live with someone like this?

ELEANOR. He's coming inside.

HELEN. How do you know?

> (*Sound of a door opening.*
>
> ELEANOR *hides behind the curtains.*
>
> *Enter* JAKE, *from the back of the house.*
>
> HELEN *immediately puts her back to a wall.*)

JAKE. Where is she?

HELEN. Where is who?

JAKE. My wife.

HELEN. She isn't here.

JAKE. I asked you where she is.

HELEN. She went home.

JAKE. Liar.

HELEN. She did. A minute ago. When she heard you at the back of the house.

> (JAKE *goes to the front door, looks out.*)

JAKE. I don't see nothing crossing that field.

HELEN. Do you think she's stupid enough to go that way? With you after her?

JAKE. Yes. I think she's about stupid enough to do anything. You got any more questions?

HELEN. No. (*Pause.*) Get out of my house. Before my husband comes back. With his gun.

JAKE. Your husband ain't coming back with any gun, honey.

HELEN. What do you mean?

JAKE. What I said.

HELEN. If you hurt Gordon—

JAKE. I haven't hurt anybody. All I want is my wife.

HELEN. Where is he?

JAKE. In the field out there. He'll be here after a while.

> (HELEN *heads toward the door, but* JAKE *intercepts her.*
>
> *He does not close on her, and she retreats to something like her former position.*)

JAKE. Take it easy baby. Take it easy. All I want is my wife. And I know she's here.

HELEN. She's not here. No one's here but me. And my husband. If you haven't killed him. (*Pause.*) Get out of here and leave me alone.

JAKE. I told you, just calm down.

HELEN. I will not calm down.

JAKE. Yes you will. Yes you will. You have to. Think about it. I mean, look at me. I'm about twice your size. And I want you to shut up. I don't want to hurt you. I just want you to shut up. Don't worry. I'm not here to bother you. Just calm down.

HELEN. Please don't hurt me.

JAKE. I won't. I won't even touch you. Tell me where my wife is and I'll leave you alone.

HELEN. Please do go.

JAKE. So what did you all do over here tonight? While I was getting my ass soaked out there, waiting for you to finish? Huh?

HELEN. We weren't doing anything.

JAKE. I bet you weren't.

HELEN. We were talking. And I made us a sandwich.

JAKE. Do you make a sandwich for every piece of white trash that crawls up to your door? You're a mighty sweet lady.

HELEN. I felt sorry for her.

JAKE. Oh, did you. And did you ask her all kinds of questions and get her to talk about me? All cow-eyed and hurt looking.

HELEN. We didn't talk about you.

JAKE. Bullshit. She was sitting right here with a bruise on her face where I knocked the hell out of her and you didn't ask her about it, you just acted like it won't there? Don't fuck with me lady, I'm not stupid.

HELEN. She didn't say anything bad.

JAKE. She told you I was drunk, didn't she? And she told you how I come home with a bottle and she told you where she hid it, but I bet she didn't tell you she poured it out. I bet she didn't tell you that's what made me so mad. I was fine up to then. That's Eleanor. That's my wife. Then she wonders why I get mad and knock the hell out of her and she gets the younguns all upset and crying and I can't stand it. Not when I been working all day to keep a mouthful of food in the house. Not when all I want is a few minutes of peace, with nobody telling me what to do. But she don't tell you about that. She just lets you see that bruise and she acts all pitiful and you don't have the sense to tell her to get the hell back home where she belongs. But I do. (*Pause.*) Is she upstairs?

HELEN. No.

JAKE. You are lying to me. Now is my goddamn wife upstairs?

HELEN. No. I told you.

JAKE. Look, ma'am. If you know what's good for you, you'll start talking to me. Or I will go up there and find her.

HELEN. I don't know. I don't know. You'll hurt her.

JAKE. I'm not going to hurt her. Not one bit. What are you looking at me like that for?

HELEN. I'm scared of you.

JAKE. I told you you don't have anything to be afraid of. I like you. Sort of respectful. You know? I mean, you got this nice house and all. Which must mean you're good people. (*Pause.*) So did you and your husband enjoy my wife? Is that why you kept her over here all night? (*Pause.*) Did you?

HELEN. I told you. We talked.

JAKE. Your husband fucked her. I know he did. He told me so. You must have been out of the room when it happened. He said they rolled all over the floor. Right in here. You probably didn't hear it, this is such a big house.

HELEN. You liar.

JAKE. I'm not lying, ma'am. It's no news to me my wife is a tramp. I'm sorry if you thought your husband was above that kind of stuff. But you might as well know.

HELEN. You are disgusting.

JAKE. So what about it? You want me and you to roll around a little?

HELEN. You stay away from me.

JAKE. Think about it now. I'm not all soft, like old Gordon is. I'm a man. A real one. You might like it, if you give it a try.

> (*Enter* GORDON, *through the front door.*
> *He has been shot in the shoulder.*
> *He carries no gun.*)

HELEN (*going to him*). Gordon.

GORDON. I'm all right.

HELEN (*seeing the wound; to* JAKE). You bastard. You did shoot him.

JAKE (*laughing; to* GORDON). Tell her. (GORDON *does not react.*) Tell her.

GORDON (*wearily*). I shot myself. I was trying to get the safety off. Out in the field.

HELEN. Shot yourself.

GORDON. Yes.

JAKE. It was a pretty sight. Yes ma'am. The whole thing was.

GORDON. Shut up.

JAKE. Your husband and me had a really touching talk. He did the talking. He had a whole lot to say about me and my family, and how people like you wish there was something you could do to help people like us. And I thought that was right sweet, that you would want to extend the hand of generosity and all. To poor folks like us. And he had a whole lot to say about you. About how sorry he was that you let yourself get involved in this whole situation. You don't have any common sense, as far as old Gordon here can tell. You got a lot of feelings, which will probably make you a good mother later on. But you don't have any common sense.

GORDON (*interjecting;* JAKE *should barely pause*). Don't listen to this crap.

JAKE. Of course he grew up in Atlanta and he understands all kind of things that are mysteries to the rest of us. (*Laughs.*) So old Gordon, he told me about all that and I just thanked him for all that information. He talked for a long time and I figured he wanted to make friends or something, after a while. Like he was real lonely. But he kept on standing there after he got through saying all that and I figured he wanted something else. In fact, I was getting a little worried.

GORDON. He wouldn't leave. He said he wouldn't. He said he was coming back in here.

JAKE (*to* HELEN). Anyway, Gordon says to me, he says, "Well, don't you think you can go on home now? Because your wife will be along in just a minute." And I says, "Well, no, I can't do that. Because I still don't have my baby." And Gordon says, "I assured you she's coming home in a minute." Assured me. (*Laughs.*) And I says, "Well Gordon, I know what you said. But I want her out here now." And he didn't like that, no sir. So he gets a little bit red in the face and he says, "Now I told you to get off my land."

GORDON. I bought this land. I own it. This is mine.

JAKE. That's pretty much what you said, all right. (*Manner changes.*) But like I told him, lady, just because he paid money for this piece of ground don't mean he knows anything about it. I hunted with my daddy all through here, all up and down this river. I been walking these woods since I was knee high. Hell, one time I shot a squirrel right where this house is standing, back before anybody ever thought of clearing out this land and putting up some shit-ass brick house. And your husband, he says, "I am telling you to get off my land before I have to use more forceful methods," or some such shit as that. And that's when he pulls out that little pistol.

(GORDON *would like to say something but is perfectly helpless at this point.*)

JAKE (*having barely paused*). So he waves this gun around and says for me to get off his land again, and I can tell from how he's holding the gun he don't a bit more know what he's doing with it than the man in the moon. So I told him he ought to put the thing away before he shoots himself. And he gets real mad and starts trying to take off the safety, and sure enough shoots himself right through the shoulder.

GORDON. I'm fine. It's just bleeding. I'm fine.

JAKE. Real brave, ain't he?

HELEN. Leave him alone. Get out of here.

JAKE. But I haven't finished telling you what happened. See. (*Gestures to* GORDON'*s shoulder, where there is a crude bandage.*) See that bandage? I put that on him. So he wouldn't bleed to death. And then I did you a big favor, lady. I threw that pistol halfway to tomorrow.

HELEN (*to* GORDON). Is that true?

GORDON. Then he left me out there. In a ditch.

JAKE. I should have thrown you in the river.

GORDON. Get out of my house before I call the police.

JAKE (*laughing*). Go ahead. Call. Then tell him all about how you blew hell out of your shoulder. Sheriff will love that.

GORDON (*rushing at* JAKE *but collapsing in the process*). Get out of my house, get out.

JAKE (*to* HELEN). This is a real man you got, lady.

HELEN. You leave him alone.

JAKE. Yes sir. He's a man. (*Pause; to* HELEN.) Now, where is my wife?

> (JAKE *stands over* GORDON, *who is doubled up with*
>   *pain.*
> JAKE *nudges* GORDON'*s injured shoulder lightly.*
> GORDON *yelps.*)

HELEN. She's not here. She left. She went home. I told you. She must be there by now.

JAKE. Don't lie to me.

> (JAKE *touches his toe to the shoulder again.*
> *When she hears* GORDON's *groan of pain,* ELEANOR
> *emerges from the curtains.*)

JAKE. Hello baby.

HELEN. Please don't hurt her.

JAKE. I'm not going to hurt her. (*To* ELEANOR, *losing all anger as he watches her.*) Hey baby.

ELEANOR. Hey Jake.

JAKE (*increasingly tender*). You act like you scared of me.

ELEANOR. I am.

JAKE. Don't be.

ELEANOR. I can't help it.

JAKE. I'm all right now. (*No response.*) You been enjoying a nice visit with these folks?

ELEANOR. I had to go somewhere.

JAKE. No you didn't.

ELEANOR. Yes I did. Jake, you hit me hard.

JAKE. Baby, no I didn't.

ELEANOR. You did. You hit me hard.

> (*Silence.*)

JAKE (*with genuine, childlike sorrow*). I'm sorry.

ELEANOR. I don't believe you are.

JAKE. Will you come home now?

ELEANOR. I'm still scared.

JAKE. I won't hit you anymore.

ELEANOR. I still don't believe you. I don't.

JAKE. Baby, I said I was sorry.

ELEANOR. You run me out in the rain. You hit me hard. You always say you won't do it again but you will. And it doesn't matter what I do, I could do exactly like you want and you would still hit me. And I'm scared of you.

JAKE. Don't say that, I don't want you to feel like that.

ELEANOR. I do.

JAKE. I promise not to do it anymore. I promise. Just please come home.

HELEN (*to* ELEANOR). You don't have to go if you don't want to.

JAKE (*with savage anger*). Lady, you shut up.

GORDON. She can. She can stay if she wants to.

(ELEANOR *cuts off* JAKE*'s reply.*)

ELEANOR. Thank you. But it's time.

JAKE. Yes it is.

HELEN. Are you sure?

ELEANOR. I can't leave my children alone all night.

HELEN. I wish you didn't have to go.

ELEANOR. He won't hit me anymore tonight.

JAKE (*to* ELEANOR). You go on home now, baby. I got something to say to these folks.

ELEANOR. No Jake, just come on with me.

JAKE (*in a harder tone*). Get on, like I said. I ain't going to bother anybody, I just want to say something to these folks.

HELEN (*to* ELEANOR). Let me get you a coat.

JAKE. She don't need a coat.

HELEN. But it's raining.

JAKE. She didn't come over here with no coat. She ain't leaving here with one. (*To* ELEANOR.) Go on. I'll be after you directly.

(ELEANOR *hesitates, goes to* HELEN, *clasps her arms but does not embrace her.*)

ELEANOR. Don't worry about me ma'am. He'll be all right.

HELEN. Take care of yourself.

JAKE (*to* ELEANOR). Go on now. Do like I told you. Get home.

>   (*Exit* ELEANOR.)

JAKE. I just want you folks to know. We probably won't live here all that long but while we do. If you see my wife on the road, don't stop to pick her up. If she comes knocking at your door, just send her home. You understand me? There ain't nothing you can do to come between me and my wife. I got my bonds on her. (*Pause; turns to* GORDON.) And you think about one more thing. If you call the sheriff. It was you pulled the gun. It might be you lands in jail. You know it? (*Pause; from exit, winking at* HELEN.) Too bad you come back so quick, Gordon. Your wife and me was just starting to get along. No telling what would have happened if you'd laid out in that mud a little while longer.

>   (*Exit* JAKE.
>
>   *Long silence.*)

HELEN (*going to window*). I already called the deputy.

GORDON. You did what? Christ, Helen.

HELEN. I already called him. He wasn't there. He's going to call me back.

GORDON. Who did you talk to?

HELEN. His wife. I didn't tell her anything. Just that there was some trouble and to have her husband call me.

GORDON. Well when he calls back you tell him there's nothing wrong.

HELEN. But you can't keep this a secret. What about your shoulder?

GORDON. My shoulder doesn't have anything to do with the deputy.

HELEN. But you have to go to a hospital.

GORDON. Please, Helen.

HELEN. Gordon, you could bleed to death.

GORDON. I'm not hurt that bad, it went through the muscle.

HELEN. Through the muscle! This is nonsense. You're going to the doctor.

(GORDON *sits on the couch, looking at his shoulder.*)

GORDON. All right. But we're going to drive to Atlanta. I will not go to some hick emergency room. You can tie it up. (*Pause.*) Don't look at me like that. I won't die. (*Pause.*) And we're going to tell them I was cleaning the gun and it went off.

HELEN. Gordon.

GORDON. Please, Helen.

HELEN. I don't lie very well, Gordon. (*Pause.*) Shall I tie up your arm? Then we'll go.

GORDON. We have to wait till the deputy calls back. (*Pause.*) You knew better than to call anyone. We had already discussed it.

HELEN. Please, Gordon.

GORDON. You couldn't trust me to handle it my way.

HELEN. When the gun went off, I didn't know what to do.

GORDON. How did he get in?

HELEN. I didn't have the back door locked.

GORDON. What happened while you were in here with him?

(HELEN *looks at him for a long time.*)

HELEN. Don't do this. Don't.

GORDON. No. It's a simple question. What happened? You were with him a long time.

HELEN. Nothing happened. Please, Gordon.

GORDON. He was in here a long time. What did he do?

HELEN. He tried to scare me. He tried to make me tell him where she was. Then you came in. (*Pause.*) That's all.

(*Silence.*

HELEN *moves to the window.*

GORDON *stands.*)

GORDON. Do you see anything?

HELEN. No. (*Pause.*) I don't know how you could ask me that question.

(*Silence.*)

GORDON. I'm sorry. It's been a long night.

HELEN. Yes it has.

(*Silence.*)

GORDON. I guess I've acted like a fool.

HELEN. Well I think you have.

(*The phone begins to ring.*

GORDON *goes to answer it at once.*)

HELEN. Now I see someone. At the window.

(GORDON *answers the phone.*)

GORDON. Hello. (*Disappointed.*) Oh, hello Jenny. Well no, Jenny, I don't think we'll get over there after all. (*Pause.*) No, it's not the storm. (*Laughs.*) Well, to tell the truth, Jenny, I shot myself. With a gun. (*Pause.*) Oh yes, it had bullets in it. Well, that's a long story, we'll tell it to you sometime. Oh I'm fine. Oh no, everything's all right, it just nicked me. Helen is going to drive me to Atlanta. (*Pause.*) Well, I don't know why Atlanta, that's just where I want to go. (*Pause.*) Well, don't worry about me, I'll be fine. Say hey to Bob. We'll call you. Take care.

(*Hangs up.*

Silence.)

GORDON. You still see her?

HELEN. There's somebody at the window. I think it's her.

GORDON. She can see you, you know.

HELEN. I know.

(*Silence.*)

GORDON. Is she still there?

HELEN. Yes.

(*Lights begin to dim.*)

HELEN. I don't think I can live here, Gordon. Not anymore.

(GORDON *moves to the window.*)

GORDON. It is a long way from the city.

HELEN. Yes it is.

(*Blackout.*)

Craig Lucas, on *Math and Aftermath*

The boundaries of self are said to blur if not vanish altogether at certain moments—death, orgasm, meditation, even sneezing. Jim Grimsley has written a play about the first two, and about the desire to get lost and the need to find oneself, which, after all, is all an ego is: boundaries. I am what you are not: over here, inside this skin, with these preferences, these desires and these fears. This is how I see myself: I am young *because* you are old. I am homosexual only in opposition to someone who is heterosexual. (If everyone were straight, there would be no need for such a designation. We do not have a word for living human beings without lungs, because there is no such thing, so there is no need to give it a word. Words are boundaries: them and us.) I am alive solely on the basis of someone's death—mine or another's.

With death, the "I" disappears. But if I have imprinted myself on the flesh of another human being, or on the retinae of many, many humans, through the medium of film or art, then I am still seen; I am felt; I am remembered. I exist. If I have never been seen—because I am queer and it is the 1950s in America—if I have never registered, then I cannot be remembered.

As death defines living, fear and loathing define desire.

Math and Aftermath—set on Bikini Atoll in the Marshall Islands on February 28, 1954, one day before the explosion of the first hydrogen bomb—juggles playfully with serious matters; it plays with death and sex, with what is seen and what is hidden (both by individuals, and by an entire nation). What place could be more lost than an uninhabited sandbar in the far-off Pacific about to be blown sky-high and rendered radioactive and uninhabitable for thousands of years? The H-bomb project was secretly funded by Congress in order to give the U.S. the capacity to destroy our enemy the Soviet "empire." In order to keep the competitive edge in scientific research, all investigations into the workings of atoms were kept hidden from the people who were paying for the research, that is, the American people; Julius and Ethel Rosenberg were electrocuted for purportedly trading such secrets to the Soviets. They were bad secret-keepers. The Federal Bureau of Investigation—for which my father worked as a secret agent in the 1950s—helped uncover the hidden American traitors: Communists and homosexuals. Thus the two were inextricably linked in the minds and imaginations of Americans as enemies. On "our" side, you had patriots and straight people, on "theirs," traitors and fags.

As E. B. White has pointed out, it takes a lot of energy to maintain an enemy. As history demonstrates, it takes nuclear energy to maintain one on the global scale.

The enemy within—the Commie, the Queer—pales in comparison with the Enemy Even Deeper Within. I'm talking about the one within the molecules of physical matter: the electrons; the radioactive isotopes; the spinning, invisible and unstable particles which at any instant can blow us all back into the heavens, back to the moment of our conception—the big bang.

Which, as Jim Grimsley has it, is the name of the gay porn movie being shot on the beach of the world's most lost place, Bikini Atoll, in 1954, on the day before the explosion of the first hydrogen bomb.

We now know, as best as it is possible to know these things, that at the instant of the big bang, "every place and every time was identical." I heard Timothy Ferris say this last night on PBS; he was talking about the moment when the entire universe was a little speck of nothing or next to nothing—an infinitesimal fraction of one second into our creation. He said, "Every place and every time was identical at the beginning of the big bang." And this is science.

So the gay filmmakers of the imagined porn classic *Big Bang* must sneak onto Bikini Atoll and hide themselves in order to make themselves visible on film to countless viewers, who will then lose themselves in the act of watching *Big Bang;* when *they* come, they will be seeing something long gone, footage shot one day before the first hydrogen bomb exploded, ripping apart every boundary of physical matter. Within the exploding atoms of a hydrogen bomb, is time itself rearranged? Would that it were possible to go back to a time before such questions could even be conceived, before there were words.

The song "Let's Get Lost" by Frank Loesser and Jimmy McHugh was recorded by Chet Baker on March 7, 1955. September 21, 1955, Jim Grimsley was born.

Scientists have suggested that when the universe finishes expanding, and can no longer support the energy moving outward and must give in to the gravitational pull, collapsing in upon itself, that time will then move in the opposite direction. Like breathing out and breathing in, we can only wonder which came first, which breath is forward and which one back. Maybe the universe is simply breathing out and breathing in, trying to lose itself in the orgasm of a big bang which will start it all again. A conception.

Mathematicians are trying to unravel the questions raised by the big bang. Their search for a unifying theory—a formula which would obliterate the boundaries between gravity and the weak force and the strong force, melding everything into one great big theory—comes closer and closer to unifying all life and time and space, which means that there will be nothing separating you from me, young from old, then from now, here from there, straight from gay, alive from dead. At that moment, we shall all be both lost and found.

MATH AND AFTERMATH

Math and Aftermath premiered at Seven Stages Theatre in Atlanta in March 1988, in a production directed by Pamela McClure, featuring Wayne Sizemore as Grip, Tim Martin as Best Boyd, Henry Lide as Pug Montreat, Don Smith as Hugh Young, Madeleine St. Romain as the Voiceover, Lane Wittemore as Dawn Stevens, Bobby Box as Joe Lube Cool, Maria Helena Dolan as Blue Donna Morgan, and Sarah Strickland as the Ghost of Hugh Young. The set was designed by Bill Georgia.

Math and Aftermath was produced in New York at the Camilla Theatre in 1995 by Harlan Productions, directed by Dean Gray, featuring Kernan Bell as Grip, David Duffield as Best Boyd, Jeff Burchfield as Pug Montreat, John-Michael Lander as Hugh Young, Elisabeth Lewis Corley as the Voiceover, Sheri Galán as Dawn Stevens, Joe Hefferman as Joe Lube Cool, Antonia Beamish as Blue Donna Morgan, and David Morgan O'Connor as the Ghost of Hugh Young. Music composition and sound were by Michael Keck; lights, by Jack Mehler; set, by Daniel Ettinger; and costumes, by Fabio Toblini.

PLAYERS

GRIP, a multitalented technician in his 30s

BEST BOYD, a technician in his 20s

PUG MONTREAT, a fading porn star, still rather good looking, in his 40s

HUGH YOUNG, a young man in his 20s, the mysterious star of *Big Bang*

VOICEOVER, the voice that occasionally states someone's thoughts. The voice should be offstage.

DAWN STEVENS, the attorney for Blue Donna Morgan and formerly the star of many straight and lesbian porn features

JOE LUBE COOL, the motorcycle-cult muscle-stud star of *Big Bang*, the continuation of his long career as gay porn's leading screen idol

BLUE DONNA MORGAN, the lesbian producer of gay porn who wrote, produced, and directed *Big Bang*

GHOST OF HUGH YOUNG

SETTING

The play takes place on February 28, 1954, on the beach at Bikini Atoll, in the Marshall Islands. 16 mm movie cameras and other kinds of recording and lighting equipment are set up around a blanket on a mound of sand. Other representations of beach foliage indicate we are outdoors on a beach. However, the amount and placement of the equipment makes this ambiguous at the same time.

> GRIP *and* BEST BOYD *are eating lunch near the blanket but not on it. They are each reading a gay porn magazine.*

GRIP. Did anybody see the ship yet?

BEST BOYD. Nope.

GRIP. Is anybody keeping watch?

BEST BOYD. Of course somebody's keeping watch. Relax.

GRIP. I just got the creeps, that's all.

BEST BOYD. Nobody can fault you for that.

GRIP. This place is so goddamn quiet.

BEST BOYD. Of course it's quiet. There's nobody here.

GRIP. I wish we would finish up and get the hell out of here.

BEST BOYD. Relax. You want to go for a swim later?

GRIP. Hell no I don't want to go for a swim.

BEST BOYD. It's a shame to waste all this beach.

GRIP. I've had enough of this beach for one lifetime. The minute I
    see that ship I'm getting my ass out of here.

BEST BOYD. It's not due here for a while.

GRIP. I don't care, I'm keeping my clothes on.

BEST BOYD. Suit yourself.

    (*They eat again in silence.*)

GRIP (*looking offstage, seeing a crowd of people*). Where's Joe? I see
    everybody else but I don't see Joe.

BEST BOYD. Probably back at the helicopter fucking the pilot, if I
    know Joe.

GRIP. Goddamn, he better not be.

BEST BOYD. You can't tell him nothing.

GRIP. If he's too tired to get it up this take I'm going to kick his ass.

BEST BOYD. Big talk. You can't kick a star.

GRIP. The hell I can't.

BEST BOYD. Blue Donna won't like that kind of talk around Joe.

GRIP. Fuck Blue Donna. If that son of a bitch keeps me here one
    minute longer than I have to be here I will kick his ass from
    both ends. Pea-brain bastard. I knew he was trying to get in
    the pilot's pants.

BEST BOYD. So were you. So was I. So was everybody.

GRIP. Prissy little stuck-up jerk.

BEST BOYD (*checking watch*). Won't be long now.

GRIP (*nervously*). What won't be long?

BEST BOYD. The end of lunch. What do you think, I'm going to sit here and let a bomb fall on us?

GRIP. I'm just edgy, that's all.

(*Enter* PUG MONTREAT.)

MONTREAT. This heat.

BEST BOYD. You said it.

MONTREAT. It's just unbelievable. I don't see how these natives in these mythical places stand it.

BEST BOYD. It must be hard.

MONTREAT. This heat and these bugs.

BEST BOYD. Of course there's nobody here anymore.

MONTREAT. True.

BEST BOYD. I walked in the village and didn't even see a lizard on a rock.

MONTREAT. I don't actually see what that's got to do with the heat.

BEST BOYD. If there were more people here to absorb the heat it would be cooler.

GRIP. I read about that.

BEST BOYD. If this place was, like, a resort, we would be absolutely air-conditioned.

GRIP. This magazine article. Maybe it was in *Time*. Or *Life*.

MONTREAT. How much longer is it?

BEST BOYD. Till what?

MONTREAT. Till we can leave.

BEST BOYD. We just got this last session on the blanket.

MONTREAT. Am I in this one?

(GRIP *stifles laughter.*)

BEST BOYD. No sweetheart, this is just Joe and you-know-who.

MONTREAT. I'm not getting very much footage in this film.

BEST BOYD. You got that nice long take in the hut.

MONTREAT. Joe was on top of me the whole time, nobody could see me.

GRIP. Let's don't talk about this shit right now, I'm trying to eat.

> (MONTREAT *sulks.*
>
> *Enter* HUGH YOUNG, *carrying a book, wearing a beach-length terry cloth robe with a hood. The hood is pulled over his head so that his whole face is in shadow; the impression should be extravagant and sinister.*
>
> HUGH YOUNG *goes to the blanket, fumbles through a bag, and finds a pack of cigarettes. This should be done quickly but not hurriedly.*
>
> *Exit* HUGH YOUNG.
>
> HUGH YOUNG *does not acknowledge the presence of the others, nor do they speak while* HUGH YOUNG *is onstage. This should be awkward, as if they have just been talking about* HUGH.)

MONTREAT. Have you seen Blue Donna?

GRIP. I don't know where she is. (*Looks at newspaper; to* BEST BOYD.) Can you believe Eisenhower?

BEST BOYD. Hell no. Can you?

GRIP. Hell no. I think the motherfucker is crazy.

BEST BOYD. Me too.

GRIP. How about Truman?

BEST BOYD. He was another crazy motherfucker.

GRIP. I sure am glad I don't look like his daughter.

BEST BOYD. God.

GRIP. You ever hear her sing?

BEST BOYD. No. Can she sing?

GRIP. Hell no.

MONTREAT. She's got to put me in this scene. I could just stand over the two of them and do a hand job.

GRIP. Sounds like a frog. Tries to sing this popular stuff.

BEST BOYD. I say, if you can't sing, don't.

GRIP. You read about this guy?

BEST BOYD. Which one?

GRIP (*pointing to a picture in the newspaper*). This guy. How do you say it? Man, he makes me nervous.

BEST BOYD. Me too.

GRIP. I mean, the creeps.

BEST BOYD. Yeah, I know.

GRIP. How do you know you're not a Communist?

BEST BOYD. Beats me. I guess you have to read these books.

GRIP. Like that Marx?

BEST BOYD. Yeah. Those guys.

GRIP. But if you read it, like, maybe, doesn't that make you look like you are one?

BEST BOYD. Best thing to do is, go in the library and read the books, and don't ever check them out. You know? Don't leave any records.

MONTREAT. I have some overdue books.

BEST BOYD. You read?

MONTREAT. Sure. Cookbooks and stuff.

GRIP. This whole thing kills me. This Communism. You know?

BEST BOYD. I don't even know what it is.

MONTREAT. It means you don't own anything yourself but everybody owns everything and they share it. I read all about it. I used to think it was pretty neat. Look, don't you think we could use a third in this shot? I mean, I know you're not creative people but don't you think I'm right? I could just stand over the blanket behind Joe and Hugh and jerk off. Just a simple, sort of a subtle hand job. I did that in *Dust in the Sand* and it worked great.

> (GRIP *mumbles something.*)

MONTREAT. Excuse me?

GRIP. I had a frog in my throat.

MONTREAT. I thought you said something.

BEST BOYD. How long ago did you make *Dust in the Sand*?

MONTREAT. That's not important. It's the concept that's important.

GRIP. Well, we're not creative people.

BEST BOYD. Yeah.

> (*The* VOICEOVER *is simply a miked voice.*
> *No actor should appear on stage to represent the*
> VOICEOVER.)

VOICEOVER. He was reading a page from the book. He had found a book on the beach, half-buried in the sand. It looked to him as if the book had dropped onto the beach out of the future and was just lying there. For anybody to pick up. So he did.

BEST BOYD. Whose thoughts are these?

GRIP. Don't look at me.

VOICEOVER. When he read the book, he felt as if he already knew everything in it, even though he had never read about nuclear theory before. It occurred to him that there was something odd about the book, something unusual. Many of the concepts seemed far in advance of the elementary science book he remembered. Sure enough, when he checked the date of the copyright, he discovered that the book had not yet been published. Following this discovery, he read the book with increased fascination.

BEST BOYD. Somebody with a book.

GRIP. Hugh Young had a book when he came in.

MONTREAT. This is incredible.

BEST BOYD. What is?

MONTREAT. I'm having the most sensational feeling right now.

BEST BOYD. Really?

MONTREAT. Yes. I can't explain it. But I have this urge to tell you all sorts of revealing things about myself. To touch your heart. To reveal myself as a fully rounded character in all my complexities. Right here, right now.

GRIP. Great.

MONTREAT. I'm serious.

GRIP. Sounds fantastic.

MONTREAT. What do we really know about each other, anyway?

BEST BOYD. I've often thought that. What do we really know?

MONTREAT. This is wonderful. This is really terrific. I feel as if I stand at some crossroads in my life, as if the events of the next few minutes could have a profound impact on me and, really, all of human history and the world. Let's talk.

BEST BOYD. What does this have to do with the book?

MONTREAT. What book?

BEST BOYD. The book we were just talking about. The one from the future—

MONTREAT. That's it. The future. I can feel my whole future stretching out in front of me. This is just the beginning. Tomorrow and tomorrow and all that. My career is not over. My life is just beginning. This is terrific. I feel this incredible sense of myself as a worthwhile person. Each moment of our lives is so fleeting. Every person we meet has something to offer. (*Looks at* BEST BOYD *and* GRIP.) Well. Say something.

GRIP. I think you would look pretty stupid jerking off behind Joe and Hugh.

MONTREAT. Pardon me, what did you say?

GRIP. You heard me.

MONTREAT. I believe I did.

> (*Blackout.*
>
> GRIP *and* BEST BOYD *lie facedown on the blanket.*
>
> MONTREAT *pulls out a screenplay and begins to study it.*
>
> *Enter* DAWN STEVENS.)

DAWN STEVENS (*to audience*). I would like to perform the following piece. (DAWN *sets up a chair or stool in a particular spot.*) Light please. (*Light comes up on the stool.*) This chair represents the mass-media consumerist culture being forced on the rest of the world by the dominant white capitalist elite. Music please.

> (*Music comes up.*
>
> DAWN *begins to move abstractly in relation to the chair or stool.*
>
> *She is attempting to take on the shape of the chair or stool but is having trouble.*
>
> *She can't get the hang of the necessary perpendiculars, cannot capture the essence of the seating device.*)

MONTREAT (*reading from the script*). You know what I want. You know what I need. Baby. I'm it. I'm the 1. For U. Look at that. Look at that stuff. That's all for U. All for U baby. Yeah. Come on. Yeah, that's it. You know what to do. You've got the touch.

Hold it. Go easy now. That's it. Nice and easy. Rough stuff comes later. Yeah. That's it. Make it smooth. Real smooth. I'll tell you about smooth some day. Oh baby. Look out. I'm almost ready. I'm almost there. Yeah, you can take it can't you. You can take it all.

DAWN. New movie?

MONTREAT. Yes. I have an audition as soon as I get home.

DAWN. Sounds like the same old shit.

MONTREAT. Pretty much.

DAWN. I don't see why they bother to write it down. What's this one called?

MONTREAT. *Hit Me with Your Hard Hat.* It has a really neat scene in the kitchen while they're making slaw.

> (*Blackout.*
>
> DAWN STEVENS *lies down on the blanket between* GRIP
> *and* BEST BOYD.
>
> *Enter* JOE LUBE COOL, *in jeans, a leather jacket,*
> *leather trappings, boots, and a leather cap*
> *pulled down over the eyes, throwing the face*
> *into shadow.*
>
> JOE LUBE COOL *faces away from the audience.*
>
> MONTREAT *kneels in front of* JOE.)

MONTREAT. Do you think this is right?

VOICEOVER. He doesn't think about it.

MONTREAT. That we treat each other like this I mean.

VOICEOVER. He doesn't think about anything. He just stands there.

MONTREAT. You know what I mean. We're supposed to be making a movie.

VOICEOVER. He looks off in the distance. He has a fantastic body. He has perfect vision. He can see the leaves of the palms far away. He can see the shadows of the leaves on the sand. He cannot see the man at his feet.

(MONTREAT *wraps himself around* JOE'S *feet*.)

MONTREAT. I think we should just talk. We have a lot to say. We have a lot to share with each other. I want to get to know you as a person. I want to experience you. I want to touch your life in a very special way, unlike anything that any lover has ever given you before. I think we should go away for the weekend. Really get away. Spend some time alone. Share some real solitude. Together. We should talk about it.

(*Blackout.*

Lights rise slowly.

JOE *has turned to face the audience.*

His face is still shadowed by the brim of the leather cap.

MONTREAT *is behind him.*

MONTREAT *embraces* JOE, *running hands beneath the leather jacket, along* JOE'S *torso*.)

MONTREAT. Are we rehearsing? (*Pause; no answer.*) What time is it? Tuesday? (*Pause; no answer.*) I love touching you like this. It reminds me of so much. So many other times. Is that right? Is that what I'm supposed to say?

(MONTREAT *steps away from* JOE LUBE COOL, *turns, and walks across* GRIP, BEST BOYD, *and* DAWN; *exit* MONTREAT.

While the VOICEOVER *speaks,* JOE *remains in light onstage, leather jacket over shoulder, torso bare.*)

VOICEOVER. He pictured them fucking. In his brain they were all naked and fucking wildly. The men and the women were coming again and again. They were screaming at the tops of their lungs. The women were totally destroyed by pleasure. The men were having fantastic orgasms that lasted almost an hour. There was a heap of them on the blanket and asses were flying. He wondered what would happen if he described something like that out loud. If he suggested something like that. Even though he was a porn star, people would be shocked. People thought that was just for the movies. People thought he was just making that up. But he really wanted to fuck like that. Fantastically. Without ever stopping.

(*Exit* JOE.

Lights rise on DAWN STEVENS *and* BLUE DONNA MORGAN.

They are having a story conference.

Everyone else is offstage.)

BLUE DONNA. All the footage with Montreat sucks so far.

DAWN. I have to agree.

BLUE DONNA. That stuff about the Bible. Jesus, where was that coming from? I mean, I know I told him to improvise but that stuff just stinks.

DAWN. I think he has a lot of hang-ups about his childhood.

BLUE DONNA. He doesn't look so bad till he opens his mouth.

DAWN. How old is he?

BLUE DONNA. God knows.

DAWN. Maybe you can do something in the editing room.

BLUE DONNA. What I ought to do is beat the motherfucker to death.

DAWN. You can cut the scene in and out of this solo scene, the one with Joe humping the motorcycle.

BLUE DONNA. That's great stuff, isn't it?

DAWN. Nobody's ever seen anything like it.

BLUE DONNA. Looks like they're joined right here. (*Indicates the pelvic region.*) God he looks fantastic.

DAWN. Joe's a star all right.

BLUE DONNA. He's worth every penny we're paying if he'd just stop fucking everything that moves.

DAWN. He's nervous.

BLUE DONNA. What's he got to be nervous about? We're paying him a fortune. I'm the one who should be nervous.

DAWN. We're all tense.

BLUE DONNA. Hugh's got some tranquilizers if you're bad off.

DAWN. I don't want pills.

BLUE DONNA (*moving closer*). What's the matter baby?

DAWN. This place. It's starting to get to me.

BLUE DONNA. Are you kidding? This place is fantastic. Look at that beach. Did you ever see such a great beach? Did you ever see such great weather?

DAWN. You know what I mean.

BLUE DONNA. You're worried about the bomb. Right?

DAWN. I wish you hadn't said anything about it. It's creepy, knowing about it before everybody else.

BLUE DONNA. Where's your sense of adventure? I think it's great.

DAWN. The queens are really nervous about it.

BLUE DONNA. You mean Grip is nervous. Boyd could give a fuck.

DAWN. Boyd is crazy.

BLUE DONNA. He's great. He's fantastic. The guy can handle anything. (*Pause.*) Hey, look, you think we ought to leave? Is that what you think?

DAWN. You mean it?

BLUE DONNA. Sure. If this thing is getting to you—if you don't think we're safe here. (*Looks at* DAWN, *shrugs.*)

DAWN. But you've invested every cent you've got.

BLUE DONNA. I want you to feel safe, baby.

DAWN. You'd do that for me? All that money?

(BLUE DONNA *shrugs again.*)

DAWN. This is great. This is fantastic. I can't believe you.

BLUE DONNA. We have something special. You know? You and me. We've got a good thing, we ought to keep it. You know? I'm crazy about you. Been like that ever since *Take a Lick on the Wild Side.* Remember? That day you stood in a tub of petroleum jelly six hours and never complained. You remember?

DAWN. How could I forget? (*Pause.*) No. You're right. We have to finish this. It's important. It's more than just the money. It's history. You know?

BLUE DONNA. Right. History.

DAWN. I mean, we're here. Right? And so is the bomb. Over there somewhere. In a plane.

BLUE DONNA. There's no plane, sweetheart.

DAWN. Well what are they going to drop it out of?

BLUE DONNA. It's on a tower. Over that way.

DAWN. You mean it's already here? (*Looks uncomfortably over that way.*) How do you know so much about this thing?

BLUE DONNA. I have my sources.

DAWN. Come on. You can trust me.

BLUE DONNA. Well. You know I was in physics, right? During the war. Well, I can't tell you what I was working on, but you have heard of Nagasaki and Hiroshima, right?

DAWN. You mean—

(BLUE DONNA *nods her head slowly.*)

DAWN. You could be a pretty dangerous person, baby.

BLUE DONNA. They didn't know I was a lesbian at the time. Hell, I didn't know I was a lesbian at the time.

DAWN. So you know about subatomic theory too? You understand the theory behind this ... device. Right? And we're safe.

BLUE DONNA. As long as we're on that boat before the bomb goes off, we'll be fine. We'll have something to tell our grandchildren about, if we have any grandchildren. (*Lights fade to black.*) I mean, where would you rather be than at the beach with a few friends? At Bikini Atoll, staring at the blue lagoon.

> (*Silence.*
> *The sound of much movement.*
> *Whispers.*
> *No attempt to rush the scene change.*
> *All the actors are onstage, in place, as if filming.*
> DAWN *is operating the camera.*
> GRIP *and* BEST BOYD *are handling lights, boom mikes, and the like.*
> MONTREAT *is undressing on the blanket.*
> JOE LUBE COOL *and* HUGH YOUNG *are standing with their backs to the audience.*
> HUGH *is still wearing the long robe with the hood.*
> JOE *is still wearing the cap with the brim pulled over his eyes.*)

BLUE DONNA. Action.

MONTREAT (*for the camera*). Yes. Yes, I am older. Yes, I am not young. But here we are. The three of us. Alone. Here. You. And you. And me.

> (MONTREAT *waits expectantly.*)

VOICEOVER. The two of them did not seem to hear the man. They were separated only by distance. They could see each other out of the corners of their eyes. But they were not aware of Montreat or his tender feelings. They watched him undress as if he were a shadow moving. As if he were a ghost, already beyond death. They could feel only each other. Their hands were not touching and yet there was a pulse, a charge, as if gravity were drawing them down together onto the blanket. They did not move. Montreat finished undressing. He watched them. He was afraid.

MONTREAT. Why are you looking at me like that? Take off your clothes.

> (*The expressions on* MONTREAT's *face make clear the fact that neither* HUGH *nor* JOE *is moving to obey.*
>
> MONTREAT *becomes embarrassed since he is the only one who is naked.*
>
> *He fumbles for a cigarette.*
>
> *Finds a lighter, drops it, finds it again.*
>
> *Decides not to light the cigarette.*
>
> *Glares at the two of them.*
>
> *Stands with his hands covering his genitals.*)

VOICEOVER (*only after all the above actions have occurred*). They were sorry that Montreat had taken off his clothes so quickly. They wished they had a robe or a towel to offer him, for comfort. He had become so confused he did not know what to do next. But they could not move to help him, they could only watch.

> (MONTREAT *begins to dress.*
>
> *He should make sounds of distress, very soft and heart-felt.*)

MONTREAT. I don't have to stay here like this.

VOICEOVER. It was true. He did not have to stay.

> (*Blackout.*
>
> *Lights rise on a new scene being filmed.*
>
> GRIP *is operating the camera.*
>
> BEST BOYD *is doing the rest of the technical work.*
>
> DAWN *and* BLUE DONNA *are embracing on the blanket.*

> *Behind them* MONTREAT *is gluing together a plastic*
> *model of a strategic bomber from the late 1950s.*
> HUGH *and* JOE *are standing in the same position but this*
> *time are facing the audience.*)

DAWN. Is this just another token lesbian scene?

> (BLUE DONNA *does not answer.*
> *They begin to kiss passionately on the blanket.*)

MONTREAT. There's something odd about that blanket. Something peculiar. That's not a normal blanket. I've been watching that blanket for some time now.

> (MONTREAT *holds up the model airplane and turns it*
> *from side to side.*)

DAWN. I think there's some old queen watching us.

> (BLUE DONNA *breaks character, looks disgusted, stands.*)

BLUE DONNA. Cut.

DAWN. What did I do?

BLUE DONNA. What did you do? Did you hear yourself?

DAWN. I said the fucking line.

BLUE DONNA. Big deal. Do me a fucking favor. Next time would you fucking try to say it with a little expression?

DAWN. I had plenty of expression.

BLUE DONNA. The living fuck you did. You're supposed to give this look. I showed you. Look at me. Like this. (*She gives the look she wants.*) You're not supposed to look like Einstein. You're not a fucking scientist. You're not fucking discovering anything. Montreat is sitting right there, everybody can see him.

DAWN. I know he is. That's what's so fucking stupid about the whole thing.

BLUE DONNA. Don't give me any more free critiques, okay?

DAWN. It's a fucking porn movie.

BLUE DONNA. I know it's a fucking goddamn porn movie.

DAWN. You think you're some kind of fucking artist.

BLUE DONNA. Look, I'm sorry I hurt your feelings.

DAWN. I don't have to put up with this crap.

BLUE DONNA. I said I was sorry. Let's do it again. Okay?

>(DAWN *nods assent.*
>
>*They resume positions as at the beginning of the scene.*)

DAWN. Is this just another token lesbian scene?

>(BLUE DONNA *does not answer.*
>
>*They begin to kiss passionately on the blanket.*)

MONTREAT. There's something odd about that blanket. Something peculiar. That's not a normal blanket. I've been watching that blanket for some time now.

>(MONTREAT *holds up the model airplane and turns it from side to side.*)

DAWN. I think there's some old queen watching us.

>(BLUE DONNA *pulls her back down and continues to kiss her.*
>
>*They begin to tear at each other's clothes as lights fade to black.*
>
>JOE LUBE COOL *and* HUGH YOUNG *are still standing as before.*)

VOICEOVER (*during the scene change, which may be partially lit*). Donna knew it would be a film for the ages. Not just for today, but for tomorrow too. She had known it since she was walking on the beach at Charleston thinking about the fine architecture in that city. While she was walking on the beach, the words "big bang" had come into her mind. This was remarkable in that the big bang theory of cosmic creation was not yet widely discussed. She was thinking of another context. She had already learned, through secret channels, of the H-bomb project, and she knew of the consequences this weapon would have for the world.

> (*During the above, a motorcycle has been rolled onstage.*
> *If a real motorcycle cannot be found, an appropriate*
>   *representation may be used.*
> *The motorcycle is placed in front of the blanket.*
> *Equipment may be moved as necessary.*
> MONTREAT *stands beside the motorcycle.*
> BLUE DONNA *is operating the camera.*)

BLUE DONNA. Action.

> (MONTREAT *begins to lick the seat of the motorcycle.*
> *For a while the scene consists of this action*—MONTREAT
>   *licking and* BLUE DONNA *filming.*
> *Enter* DAWN.)

DAWN. Was that you?

MONTREAT (*pausing but not facing* DAWN). Where?

DAWN. On the beach.

MONTREAT. I was at the beach earlier. Today.

DAWN. Were you sitting beside a blanket? A very unusual blanket?

MONTREAT. I don't recall anything about a blanket.

DAWN. You were building a model of a strategic bomber. You are obviously in possession of military secrets. At the same time, you were watching me with my lover. You, or someone who looks very much like you.

MONTREAT. You must be mistaken. I've been adoring this motorcycle most of the day.

> (*Lights rise gradually to reveal* JOE LUBE COOL *and*
>   HUGH YOUNG *standing in two different parts of the*
>   *stage that have not been used until now.*

The two are facing each other.

HUGH YOUNG *lowers the hood of the robe.*

JOE LUBE COOL *takes off the cap.*

They simply watch each other.

MONTREAT *returns to cleaning the motorcycle.*

DAWN *watches.*

Blackout onstage.

Lights linger on JOE LUBE COOL *and* HUGH YOUNG.)

VOICEOVER. They had become like gods, they were seeing and hearing things they could not possibly see or hear.

(*Lights rise as* GRIP *and* BEST BOYD *roll a long object to an area of the stage closest to the audience.*

They are wearing white lab coats and stand flanking the long object, which is covered with a painted cloth.

They are holding clipboards and stand in a vaguely military stance.

JOE *and* HUGH *are still visible.*

GRIP *is eyeing the long object nervously.*)

GRIP. This thing makes me queasy.

BEST BOYD. It's not real.

GRIP. What difference does that make? It still makes me nervous.

(GRIP *moves a step away from the object.*)

BEST BOYD. Where are you going?

GRIP. Nowhere.

BEST BOYD. Why are you standing over there?

GRIP. That thing is radioactive, right? Radioactive stuff is bad for you, right?

BEST BOYD. I'm telling you, this is nothing but a fake. (*Strips off the painted cloth to reveal a bomb, looking very real.*) Look. See? (*Taps it.*)

GRIP. Cover it up.

BEST BOYD. You need to stop being so ridiculous.

GRIP. Cover it up I said.

BEST BOYD. When you have an unreasonable fear like this you should face it.

GRIP (*facing the bomb, then sitting with his hands over his eyes*). All right. I've faced it. Now cover it up.

> (BEST BOYD *replaces the cover.*
> *Lights fade to black.*
> *Lights rise on* BLUE DONNA, *who is pacing the stage.*
> *She is not aware of the presence of* JOE *and* HUGH.
> *During the scene that follows,* JOE *and* HUGH *do not move.*)

VOICEOVER. Donna knew now that it had been a mistake to bring Montreat along, but what could she do? There were hours left before the ship would come. Montreat was becoming more and more morose. Joe was remaining calm but who knew how long that would last? With Montreat licking his boots at every turn. She knew that she herself would not long have tolerated such treatment from any woman. Joe was a man with a reputation. Then there was Hugh Young to consider. Something was going on between Joe and Hugh Young, and Donna wasn't sure she approved.

> (*Enter* MONTREAT, *totally out of control.*)

MONTREAT. You've got to give me another scene. Just one more. I can carry it. I still look pretty good. I swear you won't be sorry.

> (*Goes behind blanket.*)

I'll just stand right here. I'll watch them fuck. Joe and that boy. My beautiful big strong Joe. I know how you've got that scene set up. It's very artistic. I'll just stand right here and you can bring up a light, and when they come here, it will be just like when I was watching you and Dawn.

BLUE DONNA. You know that won't work, Montreat. I can't repeat myself like that.

MONTREAT. But you've got to, you've got to give me another scene. I just need a chance. I can still work. I can still do it. They still love me, they still want me to take off my clothes. Look, I'm getting back in shape. I've been doing sit-ups all morning. Look. Look how flat. (*Shows his stomach.*)

BLUE DONNA. Joe and Hugh don't need you in the scene, they can carry it themselves.

> (*Suddenly* MONTREAT *becomes aware that* JOE *and*
> HUGH *are onstage.*
> *But he does not approach them.*
> *In some way, their placement in the separate playing*
> *areas has exalted them beyond his reach.*)

MONTREAT. Let me fuck Joe instead of Hugh, let me. Just in this one scene.

BLUE DONNA (*exiting in disgust*). You must be out of your mind. Nobody wants to watch you fuck Joe.

> (MONTREAT *gazes round in a daze.*
> *Sees the bomb.*
> *The sight of the bomb helps to sober* MONTREAT.
> *He moves toward the bomb with sudden dignity, the*
> *likes of which he has not shown before.*
> *He circles the bomb, which is covered.*
> *He pause at the nose of the bomb.*)

MONTREAT. I understand it all now.

> (*He slowly, sensuously removes the cover from the bomb.*
> *During the speech that follows, he is calm and dignified.*)

This is a three-stage bomb. The first stage is a standard fission bomb composed of a rare isotope of uranium, U-235, which constitutes only seven-tenths of one percent of all naturally occurring uranium. This isotope is inherently more unstable than the naturally occurring uranium 238, and when a sufficient quantity of a sufficient purity of the isotope is brought together in what is known as a critical mass, a fission explosion occurs.

(*In some way, perhaps by turning toward him*, MON-TREAT *acknowledges* JOE LUBE COOL.)

This atomic explosion is the first stage of the hydrogen bomb. The second stage of the explosion process occurs in the two-hundred-plus pounds of a compound called lithium deuteride placed in the vicinity of the fifty-million-degree centigrade temperatures generated by the fission explosion. Lithium 6, a light-metal isotope, produces tritium when bombarded by free neutrons such as those produced by a fission explosion. The tritium atoms are fused with deuterium atoms, combined with the lithium 6 in the lithium deuteride, by the high temperatures occurring near the fissioning uranium.

(*In some way, perhaps by turning toward him*, MON-TREAT *acknowledges* HUGH YOUNG.)

This completes the second stage of the three-stage explosion process. As a result of this stage, high-energy neutrons are released, and these neutrons cause the fission of the bomb's final component, a layer of cheap, common uranium 238 which is wrapped around the fusion bomb. This final stage of the three-stage explosion process generates more than half of the bomb's incredible explosive power and is responsible for the vast majority of the bomb's fallout generation. The fusion explosion itself is relatively clean and generates no new radio-active isotopes.

(MONTREAT *bows to* JOE LUBE COOL *and* HUGH YOUNG.) The bomb is much more powerful than the scientists have dreamed today. In the previous test of a hydrogen explosive, code-named Mike and taking place on Eniwetok, another of the Marshall Islands, a large explosive device consisting of liquid, refrigerated tritium and a central fission or atom bomb, weighing some sixty-five tons, was exploded on November 1, 1952. The bomb presently here on Bikini Atoll, which will explode sometime tomorrow over Bikini Atoll, is the first to employ the outer shell of U-238, and will usher in the age when humans can destroy whole cities at one stroke. The bomb will prove so successful, generating more than twice the expected explosive power, that a test of an even more powerful explosive a few days from now will be canceled. Neither Joe Lube Cool nor Hugh Young understands any of this. They are simply here to film a gay porn movie.

> (MONTREAT *pulls a gun from his pocket, sits down by the bomb, and shoots himself in the mouth.*
>
> JOE LUBE COOL *and* HUGH YOUNG *come down from the areas of the stage they are separately inhabiting.*
>
> *They look at* MONTREAT*'s body.*
>
> HUGH YOUNG *pulls up the hood of his robe; exit* HUGH YOUNG.
>
> JOE LUBE COOL *remains onstage until* BEST BOYD *and* GRIP *rush in.*)

BEST BOYD. I thought I heard a gun.

JOE LUBE COOL. You did.

BEST BOYD. What happened?

JOE LUBE COOL (*indicating the body*). Montreat's dead. He shot himself.

BEST BOYD. I didn't even know he had a gun.

JOE LUBE COOL (*exiting in the same direction as* HUGH YOUNG). He probably didn't have one. Until he thought about shooting himself, I mean.

> (*Exit* JOE LUBE COOL.
>
> DAWN *and* BLUE DONNA *enter and sink down onto the blanket, kissing and making love with their hands.*
>
> *At the same time,* GRIP *and* BEST BOYD *run to the bomb and find* MONTREAT.
>
> GRIP *and* BEST BOYD *simply look at each other and say nothing.*
>
> *After a while they walk around the bomb, passing each other, and look at* MONTREAT *from the other side.*
>
> *They should let a good while pass before they speak.*)

BEST BOYD. Should we drag him off somewhere?

GRIP. What for?

BEST BOYD. So we don't have to look at him.

> (GRIP *shrugs.*
>
> *They drag* MONTREAT *offstage after* BEST BOYD *puts a cloth under* MONTREAT*'s bloody head.*
>
> *Lights fade to black.*)

VOICEOVER. They were each watching. Each knew what was going on. Montreat had killed himself without any warning. The others didn't care. Secretly, each had wished the old queen dead. Some more than once, given the last few days. The filming session on the beach had taken on a timeless feeling. At first the location had seemed like a lark but after a few days the thought of the bomb made it terribly real. The heat, the sand, the glimmering lagoon in which no one could swim for fear of being seen. The horrible nights, moving from place to place with the equipment. Setting up the tents by moonlight. The sound of the helicopters, the patrol boats, the fierce glare of the searchlights. Hiding, always hiding. All for a porn movie. Blue Donna was crazy and they all knew it. She was obsessed with her movie, but they could forgive her for that. After all, they were in it. It was Pug Montreat they hated. It was Pug Montreat who whined and complained, who fussed about the sand, who couldn't eat fish, who made eyes at Joe Lube Cool and pouted whenever Joe paid attention to Hugh Young. Everyone watched Grip and Best Boyd drag his body back into the palms where soon it would be pulverized by nucleic shrapnel. While they sailed away on the *Lucky Dragon* bound for postwar Japan.

(*Lights rise on* BLUE DONNA *and* DAWN STEVENS, *who are holding scripts.*)

Only a few days before, at the beginning of the shoot, everything had seemed so much simpler. Blue Donna had seemed invincible with her mysterious ties to the Atomic Energy Commission and her knowledge of the bomb. She and Dawn Stevens had held one exciting story conference after another. The idea of *Big Bang* hovered between them. The air was charged. Anything seemed possible.

(DAWN *and* BLUE DONNA *cover the bomb.*)

BLUE DONNA. Actually, it hasn't been that hard. You're just taking a picture of a dick. Basically, I mean. If you pick out a good one and you take a good picture, you're, well, about halfway there, actually. I mean, guys don't do much for me but that works to my advantage. You know? I'm, well, not involved. Also, because I'm not all that interested in penises I don't rely on them all that much. In my films, I mean. Like, I find a guy who's pretty good looking instead of one of these pimply types. The gross maggot type, you know. With nothing but a big dick to his name and God help him. Well, I don't go for that. I look at it like, well, like something that ought to be really beautiful and sort of abstract. I mean, you never actually see anybody dressed like Joe Lube Cool. Except in LA. You know? And if you do, you never believe in them. Basically, I mean. You keep seeing this image. Well, the image is still there, I just take a picture of it. This movie is the first time I've had any lesbians in my films. I'm finding it much more difficult to deal with. (*Pause.*) What made you quit making movies girl? You were really hot.

DAWN. Thanks.

BLUE DONNA. I loved you in *Oceans of Love* and I thought you were incredible in *Starving for Your Love*, you had like this intense quality. This hunger, you know? You were, like, devouring things all the time.

DAWN. That was a really hard film to make.

BLUE DONNA. Who were your costars? I can't remember. Tomika Tamara and Kiki Dove?

DAWN. Close. Tomika and Vandra Venandra. She was a total knock-out. God. And this man. What was his name? Rod LaRue? LaRock? That's it. Rod LaRock. God, that was a long time ago. Hardly anybody ever talks about that one.

BLUE DONNA. Oh, I loved it, I thought it was an incredible perfor-mance. So answer my question. Why did you give it up?

DAWN. Let's just say I needed a change. But it's good to be doing this one. With you, I mean. (*Touches* BLUE DONNA *somewhat suggestively.*) The movie business is different than it was in my time. You know? These girls you've got are stars. I mean, look at Joe.

BLUE DONNA. Ego queen. He's had every social disease known to mammals. Every time I want him to work I have to get the health department to certify him. I tell them I'm a caterer and he's my head waiter.

DAWN (*drolly*). That's a scream.

BLUE DONNA. Hugh Young, on the other hand, is an angel.

DAWN. He is pretty.

BLUE DONNA. I could just lick his face right off.

DAWN. I've been meaning to talk to you about that.

BLUE DONNA. What? Hugh?

DAWN. You're getting obsessed with him.

BLUE DONNA. I'm not the only one. I think Joe's infatuated with him.

DAWN. Joe's going to fuck that boy and I don't mean on-screen. And when he does Montreat is going to blow sky-high.

BLUE DONNA. I thought I could just hold Pug's hand and get him through all this but I don't think I'm going to be able to do it. He's driving me out of my mind.

DAWN. You cast him. I begged you not to do it.

BLUE DONNA. Give me a break. He used to be really good. He used to be a hot man.

DAWN. He should have got out of this business a long time ago.

BLUE DONNA. He's right for this part. He's great for it. You have to admit that.

DAWN. Yeah, but the part's not good for him. He can't deal with it. He can't just watch like that. Not the two of them. I don't even know if I could.

BLUE DONNA. He has to. That's the whole point. What he remembers when he looks at them. That. And the bomb.

DAWN. Montreat is the bomb, baby. And he's going to blow. You watch.

BLUE DONNA. Maybe. But he's sure not the only one.

(*Enter* GRIP, *with bloody hands.*)

GRIP. Is this the right time?

VOICEOVER. Warning, you are about to enter a flashback.

(*Lights begin to dim on* BLUE DONNA *and* DAWN
STEVENS.
GRIP *stops short of the flashback zone.*
As the lights go out, DAWN STEVENS *lies facedown on
the blanket, and* BLUE DONNA *steps forward to join*
GRIP.)

BLUE DONNA. It's all right. We're pretty much finished.

GRIP (*holding up his hands*). We've got a problem.

BLUE DONNA. You should wash your hands.

GRIP. Yes, I know. Listen. We have a problem. I think there's something wrong around here.

BLUE DONNA. Montreat killed himself, if that's what you mean.

GRIP. It's worse than that. It's everything. I feel as if reality may be distorted, locally. Right here, I mean. Because of what's about to happen. Maybe we're actually already in the future. I'm not sure what year this is, are you? Maybe this is not even the real beach.

BLUE DONNA. Then what is it?

GRIP. The ghost of the beach. After the bomb. You know.

BLUE DONNA. You're dreaming, kid.

GRIP. Just listen. I mean, you're dealing with fundamental forces, right? Just a few hours from now. Everything unravels, right?

Over there somewhere. Right? I mean, it's just a little bomb but who's to say it doesn't work, like, backward and forward? Maybe it just bends things. Maybe.

BLUE DONNA. Since when is everybody an expert on subatomic theory? You people kill me.

GRIP. Joe says he doesn't think Montreat really had a gun. He says he thinks Montreat only got the gun after he decided to kill himself. The gun just came. Just appeared.

BLUE DONNA. Because of the bomb.

GRIP. Yes.

BLUE DONNA. Look, don't you think it's a little early to start blaming the bomb for everything? It doesn't blow up till tomorrow.

GRIP. But that doesn't matter, if it works backward. In time, I mean. You know?

BLUE DONNA. No. I don't know. Just shut up, why don't you.

GRIP. You should listen to me. I might be right. (*Laughs.*) I bet Montreat won't stay dead. What you want to bet. Not here. Not so close to that. (*Points to the bomb.*)

BLUE DONNA. Crap. That's a model. It can't do anything. (*Pause; looks around.*) It's about time we got this goddamn movie started up again. Where is everybody?

> (*Enter* BEST BOYD, *with bloody hands.*
> *He is carrying a leather flight jacket.*)

BEST BOYD. I'm afraid I've had to kill the pilot.

> (*As the* VOICEOVER *speaks, all the actors do exactly as
> the voice describes.*)

VOICEOVER. This was too much for them. They stared blankly at one another, even Dawn Stevens, who had been lying face-down on the blanket.

BEST BOYD. It was the only thing I could do. He saw me with Montreat's body. He was on the radio trying to call the Atomic Energy Commission. I had to stop him.

BLUE DONNA. Did you damage the helicopter?

BEST BOYD. No.

GRIP. How is Montreat?

BEST BOYD. Still dead.

BLUE DONNA. How did you kill the pilot?

BEST BOYD. I stabbed him from behind.

BLUE DONNA. I didn't know you carried a knife.

> (BEST BOYD *moves away, as if avoiding the question.*
> *Searches for the knife briefly, but cannot find it.*)

BEST BOYD. I'm sure it's all right. The pilot will be fine. He's going to heaven. I know, because he had a cross around his neck.

BLUE DONNA. I'm sure you're right.

GRIP. Something's wrong. It's real bad right now. There's, like, this waveform of unreality coming through here. I can feel it.

DAWN. It's like a ripple, isn't it?

GRIP. Yes, that's exactly right.

DAWN. Distortions in the fabric of space-time. The result of nuclear decay and general atomic instability in the region of the artificial fusion occurrence that's about to happen. The whole temporal region of Bikini Atoll is quivering like five-dimensional Jell-O.

BEST BOYD. That's why I had to kill the pilot.

DAWN. Exactly.

GRIP. We should all go look at Montreat and make sure he's still dead.

BEST BOYD. I told you, he was still dead just a few minutes ago.

BLUE DONNA. Have you seen Joe or Hugh?

BEST BOYD. Joe was asleep in the tent, last time I looked. I don't know where Hugh is.

BLUE DONNA. Go wake up Joe. Tell him to get his ass here. Tell him to find Hugh.

BEST BOYD. What if he doesn't know where Hugh is?

BLUE DONNA. Do what I said. Now. We've got to film this scene and get the fuck out of here.

DAWN. We don't have a helicopter anymore.

BEST BOYD. I never touched the helicopter. It's still right there.

BLUE DONNA. Can anybody fly it?

BEST BOYD. Joe can.

GRIP. No shit. He's a pilot?

BLUE DONNA. Did that jerk get through to the AEC? On the radio?

BEST BOYD. No. I don't think so. I turned it off anyway.

BLUE DONNA. We've got to move. Jesus Christ. We're going to do this scene and get out of here.

> (BLUE DONNA *paces around the blanket, intense and furious.*
>
> *She has an idea.*)

BLUE DONNA. This is fantastic. This is fate. This is just what the scene needs. (*To* GRIP.) Go drag Montreat back in here.

GRIP. What?

DAWN. Are you out of your mind?

BLUE DONNA. He wanted to be in this scene. All right, what the fuck? Drag him back in here.

GRIP. I ain't touching him.

BLUE DONNA. Bring the pilot too. We'll have dead bodies everywhere. This is incredible. This is better than the stair scene in *Potemkin.*

GRIP. I mean it, Donna. I won't touch the sucker. Don't push me.

BLUE DONNA. I'll give you a hundred dollars cash as soon as you get back.

> (*Exit* GRIP.)

DAWN. As your attorney I feel compelled to warn you that you are risking considerable liability in this matter.

> (BLUE DONNA *is checking the cameras and sound-*
> *recording equipment to make sure everything is*
> *functional.*
> *She continues to do this busily, ignoring* DAWN.
> DAWN *stares at the bomb.*)

VOICEOVER. Dawn was terrified. She had never before been faced by such a collection of bizarre circumstances. She found herself staring at the painted sheet covering the bomb. She was oddly detached from her confusion while she stared at the lurid colors of the sheet. Then she remembered that Montreat was dead and that Best Boyd had stabbed the pilot in the back, and she became upset again. But none of her emotion showed. She was remembering what it had been like to make love to Blue Donna. On her lips was the taste of Blue Donna's starved kisses. Dawn licked the taste from her lips and relished it. She was remembering Blue Donna naked in the tent, and then suddenly the image changed to Montreat with the big hole in his skull, and then Montreat sat up and started playing with another model airplane. Then the image vanished. Dawn became more afraid, realizing that she herself was now close to madness.

BLUE DONNA. Are you just going to stand there?

DAWN. I keep seeing Montreat.

BLUE DONNA. What do you mean, you keep seeing him? I'm not your analyst, I don't care what you keep seeing. Make sure that camera's right. Grip will be back any minute. I want to get a shot of him dragging in the bodies.

> (DAWN *does as she has been told.*

Near the camera, however, she finds a book.

She lifts it, opens it.)

DAWN (*to* BLUE DONNA). Is this yours?

BLUE DONNA. Would you quit fucking around?

DAWN. No, I'm serious. (*Holds up the book.*) This is about the bomb.

BLUE DONNA. How can it be about the bomb, nobody knows about it.

DAWN (*making it physically obvious that she is reading the title*). Big Bang on Bikini.

(BLUE DONNA *takes the book and examines it.*)

BLUE DONNA (*after examining the copyright page*). That explains it. The copyright date is 1965. It hasn't been published yet. (*Reads from the book.*) "An unanticipated shift in the wind, toward the south where lay inhabited islands of the Marshall group, carried fallout toward the very sectors the scientists had sought to protect. In the path of the fallout lay a navy destroyer, the islands Rongelap, Utirik and Rongerik, and a fishing boat."

(*She looks shocked and begins to search through the pages.*)

Doesn't this goddamn thing have an index?

(*Continues to search, scanning pages.*)

DAWN. What's wrong?

BLUE DONNA (*throwing down the book*). Oh Christ Jesus.

DAWN. You really have lost your mind.

BLUE DONNA. It doesn't give the name of the fishing boat.

DAWN. Well what do you need to know that for?

BLUE DONNA. Because it's a goddamn fishing boat that's supposed to pick us up. And we've got to sail south because the north is crawling with scientists.

DAWN. Well can't you talk to the captain?

BLUE DONNA. What am I supposed to tell him? That I've had this premonition that this horrible catastrophe is going to happen from a bomb that nobody even knows about yet? Jesus, I can't believe this.

DAWN. The book is probably a fake, some kind of a joke.

(*Enter* HUGH YOUNG, *unseen.*
He is still wearing the robe. He pulls down the hood.)

BLUE DONNA. Who would print a book with the copyright date 1965? Who? No, this is another one of those, those whatcha-macallits, those distortion things.

(HUGH YOUNG *advances so that they see him.*)

HUGH YOUNG. I was reading it.

BLUE DONNA. Where did you get it?

HUGH YOUNG. On the beach. Two nights ago.

(*Lights change, isolating a playing area for the*
flashback.)

VOICEOVER. She remembered now. Their conversation two nights ago. How strange and distracted Hugh Young had seemed. In the moonlight they had walked along the beach. Talking about Montreat, who had tried to strangle Hugh that afternoon be-tween takes. Had Hugh been carrying the book even then? She didn't remember.

(HUGH YOUNG *and* BLUE DONNA *enter the flashback*
zone.
HUGH *is carrying the book.*)

BLUE DONNA. The last time I worked with him was *Jealous Jet Fighter;* he wasn't like this.

(HUGH *says nothing, walks ahead of* BLUE DONNA.)

BLUE DONNA. You're sure he was choking you?

HUGH YOUNG. Yes.

BLUE DONNA. You can't blame him for being jealous, really.

HUGH YOUNG. I'm not upset. I just wish he wouldn't try to kill me.

BLUE DONNA. He was Joe's lover for years. It's hard to watch you and Joe falling in love like this.

HUGH YOUNG. I don't feel anything for Joe.

BLUE DONNA. That's not the way it looks.

(HUGH *examines the book.*)

HUGH. Pug had no reason to choke me.

BLUE DONNA. No, he didn't.

HUGH. He's going to kill himself. He's going to shoot himself in the mouth. You watch.

BLUE DONNA. Montreat couldn't even pick up a gun, much less pull the trigger.

(HUGH *moves his lips while he reads from the book.*)

BLUE DONNA (*after watching* HUGH *read for a moment*). Look, I won't let him hurt you. All right? You don't have to worry about that. You just look after yourself with Joe.

HUGH YOUNG. Why are you worried about that?

BLUE DONNA. He's a son of a bitch. He's a snake. He'd fuck the knot on a log.

(HUGH *goes on reading the book.*)

BLUE DONNA. Are you fucking him yet? I mean, besides in the movie.

HUGH YOUNG. Yes.

BLUE DONNA. Have you fucked him today?

HUGH YOUNG (*deadpan, matter-of-factly*). Yes. Twice.

BLUE DONNA. Christ. How am I supposed to get a movie out of you when you're making love to each other offscreen all the time?

HUGH YOUNG. I won't have any problem.

BLUE DONNA. You are so beautiful.

> (HUGH *goes on reading.*
>
> BLUE DONNA *becomes embarrassed by what she has just said.*)

BLUE DONNA. You know what I mean by that don't you? A presence. Something wonderful. I can't explain it. But it's what I look for. When I'm making a movie like this. Your cock's not so big but who cares? You've got something else. The camera just eats you up. Gets everything you're thinking. It's beautiful. It's just great.

HUGH YOUNG. Thanks.

BLUE DONNA. Are you just shy or am I boring the shit out of you?

> (HUGH *looks at her as if she is speaking Chinese and he is not very curious about what she said.*)

BLUE DONNA. I just like to talk to people. And this place is so weird.

HUGH YOUNG. It won't be here very much longer will it?

BLUE DONNA. What won't?

HUGH YOUNG. This island. Once the bomb goes off.

BLUE DONNA. I don't think it's quite that strong.

HUGH YOUNG (*closing the book*). Oh, I think it is. (*Pause.*) I'm very tired. I'm sorry. I'm going back to the tents.

BLUE DONNA. I think I'll just stand out here for a while.

HUGH YOUNG. All right. Good night.

BLUE DONNA. Good night.

> (*Exit* HUGH YOUNG.
>
> BLUE DONNA *stands perfectly still.*
>
> *She is very sad and cries a little—a very little, lightly.*
>
> *Lights fade.*)

VOICEOVER (*only as lights fade*). She had never been so sad before. She feels stupid. She wants to wallow in the sand and get wet.

She hates the movie and everything connected with it. They had made love twice today and would probably do it again. She wanted to be there with her camera the next time, but she knew that would be impossible. She wanted to make love to Hugh Young herself, but she knew—

BLUE DONNA. I can speak for myself.

(BLUE DONNA *says nothing, gets uncomfortable, and leaves the flashback zone.*)

VOICEOVER. She was uncomfortable. She could not think of anything to say. They had fucked twice. They would do it again.

(*Blackout.*

The following conversation takes place in the dark.)

JOE LUBE COOL. So you don't feel anything for me. Is that right?

HUGH YOUNG. Yes, that's right.

JOE LUBE COOL. Nothing at all. Not even right now?

HUGH YOUNG. Yes, that's right.

(*Silence for a moment.*)

HUGH YOUNG. So you're a son of a bitch and a motherfucker. Is that right?

JOE LUBE COOL. Oh yeah.

HUGH YOUNG. You're not even ashamed of it. You're just a piece of shit. Right?

JOE LUBE COOL. Right.

(*Silence.*)

HUGH YOUNG. They think we're fucking each other.

JOE LUBE COOL. You're shitting.

HUGH YOUNG. No, they really do.

(JOE *laughs.*)

HUGH YOUNG. They certainly don't think it's very funny.

(*Silence.*

Lights rise on BEST BOYD, *onstage alone.*

BEST BOYD *is decorating the bomb with blue and pink ribbons, lacing them crisscross over the bomb's surface.*

He does this in silence for some moments.

Enter GRIP.)

GRIP. Where is everybody?

BEST BOYD. Search me. Blue Donna was in a flashback just a minute ago, then she disappeared.

GRIP. Montreat's gone.

BEST BOYD. Where?

GRIP. I don't know.

(BEST BOYD *goes on with work on the bomb.*)

GRIP. Don't you understand what I'm telling you? Montreat's not where we left him.

BEST BOYD. I heard you.

GRIP. But he's dead.

BEST BOYD. I know. Don't get so excited.

GRIP. He didn't come back here?

BEST BOYD. No. Not yet anyway.

GRIP. You think he will?

BEST BOYD (*shrugging*). Not much of anywhere else to go.

GRIP. I should tell Joe. And Hugh.

BEST BOYD. What for?

GRIP. He's probably looking for them.

BEST BOYD. He's dead. He's probably not looking for anybody.

(BEST BOYD *has a disturbing thought.*)

BEST BOYD. Was the pilot still there?

GRIP. Yeah. Just lying there.

BEST BOYD. Good. I wouldn't want two of them walking around.

That could be pretty bad. (*Pausing in the work on the bomb.*) Don't you think this looks nice now?

GRIP. What? That thing? I think it looks pretty stupid. Did you put that shit all over it?

BEST BOYD. Now it's pretty. Don't you think so?

GRIP (*pacing*). I need a beer. We got any beer left?

BEST BOYD. Pretty soon they'll be everywhere. These, I mean. Pointing straight up. Just sitting there. I think I need to comb my hair. Do I? It feels tangled.

GRIP. Looks fine.

BEST BOYD. Do you have a comb? With you?

> (*Enter* JOE LUBE COOL.)

GRIP. Sure, back in the tent. You want to go get it, fine.

BEST BOYD (*to* JOE). Do you have a comb?

JOE LUBE COOL. Sure.

BEST BOYD. Can I borrow it?

> (JOE LUBE COOL *pulls out the comb, studies it.*
> *Throws it to* BEST BOYD.
> *Something in* JOE's *stance should indicate that he is*
> *horny.*)

GRIP. Have you seen Hugh?

JOE LUBE COOL. You talking to me? What do you want to know for?

GRIP. I need to warn him. Montreat's looking for him.

JOE LUBE COOL. I'm sure he knows that.

GRIP. But Montreat's dead.

JOE LUBE COOL (*shrugging*). What difference does that make? (*To* BEST BOYD.) Hey kid. You got that bomb looking pretty good.

BEST BOYD. Thanks.

JOE LUBE COOL. Blue Donna tell you to do that? For the movie?

BEST BOYD. No.

JOE LUBE COOL. Hey, that's great. Initiative.

BEST BOYD. I like this kind of stuff.

JOE LUBE COOL. You got a real talent for it.

> (JOE *moves very close to* BEST BOYD.
>
> GRIP *is figuring out what* JOE *is up to and begins to look uncomfortable.*)

JOE LUBE COOL. You got any black ribbon here?

BEST BOYD. Maybe, a little piece. Why?

JOE LUBE COOL (*removing his motorcycle jacket*). I want you to tie a piece of it right here. (*Points to the bicep nearest* BEST BOYD.) I think it would look great. Don't you?

> (BEST BOYD *searches for the ribbon, finds it.*
>
> *Cuts off a length of it.*
>
> *Fits it to* JOE'*s arm.*
>
> *Tenderly ties it there, touching the bicep worshipfully.*)

JOE LUBE COOL (*flexing*). Yeah. I like that. Don't you?

BEST BOYD. Yeah.

> (*They are moving closer to each other.*)

JOE LUBE COOL. You got any more initiatives?

BEST BOYD. Sure. Some.

GRIP (*to* BEST BOYD). We're about to start shooting again, you can't fuck him right now.

> (JOE *kisses* BEST BOYD *tenderly, a romantic 1950s-leading-man kiss.*
>
> JOE *continues to seduce* BEST BOYD.
>
> *Enter* BLUE DONNA, *holding a camera, followed by* DAWN STEVENS, *either nude or creatively undressed.*
>
> DAWN *is dragging a pad on which* MONTREAT'*s body is lying.*)

BLUE DONNA (*seeing* GRIP). Get over here and help Dawn.

DAWN. Please, this bastard is heavy.

> (GRIP *takes the corner of the pad farthest from the*
> *camera.*)

BLUE DONNA (*looking through the camera*). That won't work. Take off your pants.

GRIP. Look, I'm not in this fucking movie.

BLUE DONNA. All I want is your feet. But you can't have pants on.

> (GRIP *takes off pants.*)

GRIP. Where did you find him? (*Indicates* MONTREAT.)

BLUE DONNA. Right beside the pilot. Where you left him.

GRIP (*looking suspiciously at the body*). Wait a minute. I was just there and this fucker was gone.

BLUE DONNA (*shrugging*). We must have gotten there ahead of you. We were coming out of a flashback. You know how that goes.

GRIP (*nodding, as if this makes perfect sense*). What was the flashback?

BLUE DONNA (*looking uncomfortable*). We don't have time for this chatter. Pull the body and shut up.

DAWN. You sure got some ugly legs.

GRIP. Kiss my ass, why do you think I'm wearing long pants at the beach?

> (GRIP *and* DAWN *pull* MONTREAT *behind the blanket to*
> *the same position he occupied when he watched*
> DAWN *and* BLUE DONNA.
>
> *During this time,* JOE *and* BEST BOYD *have been making*
> *out quietly, but now they begin to giggle.*)

BLUE DONNA (*seeing* JOE *for the first time*). I will be goddamn.

DAWN. What?

BLUE DONNA. Will you look at that son of a bitch. Joe. Joe. Hey Joe. Break it up.

JOE LUBE COOL (*turning to look at her but not releasing* BEST BOYD). Yeah?

BLUE DONNA. Knock it off. I need him. We're about to get started again.

> (JOE *pats* BEST BOYD *on the head, kisses him tenderly another moment or two, then steps away from him. The other actors do not hold for this.*)

DAWN (*indicating the position of the body*). You like that? Or should we prop him up some.

BLUE DONNA. Leave him flat like that. It makes him look more dead.

DAWN (*wrinkling her nose*). You don't have to worry about that.

BLUE DONNA. People won't be able to smell him on the screen.

> (BLUE DONNA *checks to make sure* JOE *has obeyed her.*
> JOE *puts on the leather jacket.*
> BEST BOYD *sits dejectedly near the bomb.*)

GRIP (*fiddling with equipment; to* BEST BOYD). Get over here and help me with this.

BEST BOYD (*seeing* MONTREAT *for the first time; to* GRIP). I thought you said he was missing.

GRIP. Donna already had him. I guess.

BEST BOYD (*to* BLUE DONNA). Do you want the pilot?

BLUE DONNA. No, you cut him up too bad. He looks disgusting.

BEST BOYD. Sorry. (*Looks at* MONTREAT *again.*) I guess he wasn't looking for Hugh after all.

BLUE DONNA. Where is Hugh?

JOE LUBE COOL. He's around.

BLUE DONNA. Well find him, we don't have all day.

> (*No one is sure who should go, so no one moves.*)

BLUE DONNA. Go find him, Grip.

(*Enter a figure in a robe identical to* HUGH YOUNG's.

This is the GHOST OF HUGH YOUNG.)

GHOST. If you're looking for me, I'm here.

(*Everyone pauses and turns to the* GHOST.)

BLUE DONNA. We're ready to start shooting again.

GHOST. Is this the last scene?

BLUE DONNA. Yes. The one on the blanket. You and Joe.

(*The* GHOST *moves to center stage and holds there.*

JOE *starts to move toward him but hesitates,*

reconsiders.)

GHOST. Why are we shooting it again?

BLUE DONNA. We're not. This is the last scene. Remember? You and
Joe on the beach.

GHOST. I remember. We shot it yesterday.

(*The* GHOST *wanders to the blanket, walks around* MON-
TREAT.)

BLUE DONNA. We weren't here yesterday. Come on, let Dawn get
you in makeup.

GHOST. We shot this scene yesterday. I won't do it again.

(BLUE DONNA *does not expect this kind of behavior from*
HUGH *and is puzzled.*)

BLUE DONNA. What's got into you?

(*Enter* HUGH YOUNG, *in robe, hood down.*)

HUGH YOUNG. Are we ready to shoot yet?

(*Everyone turns, freezes.*

Each backs away from the GHOST.

JOE LUBE COOL *moves quickly to embrace* HUGH YOUNG

protectively.)

BLUE DONNA (*to the* GHOST). Who are you?

GHOST (*pointing to* HUGH YOUNG). Him.

(*The* GHOST *moves slowly toward* HUGH.

Anyone in the GHOST*'s path backs away.*

HUGH *shows no fear, nor does he acknowledge* JOE*'s
presence.*

The GHOST *stops some distance from* HUGH.)

GHOST. Hugh Young.

HUGH YOUNG. Yes?

GHOST. Hello.

HUGH YOUNG. Hello.

(*The* GHOST *lowers hood.*

Lights should be dim enough that his head glows.

*He is hairless and smooth of feature, and he has no
mouth.*

The GHOST *approaches* HUGH *and* JOE.

HUGH *stares at the* GHOST, *fascinated.*

JOE *quickly leads* HUGH *beyond the* GHOST *to the vicinity of the blanket.*

The GHOST *goes to the bomb.*

*He removes his robe, revealing a full-body costume that
glows.*

The GHOST *moves around, over, and under the bomb as
he speaks.*)

GHOST. I want to be in the movie. With this. This is the scene I
want to film, where I am with this, and me and this are everything. You know? So get your camera and film me. Make a
record of this. It was good for me, to live through the bomb.
You know? Now I know so much more. I come all to pieces
just thinking about it. Now I know what I want. I want this. I
want to dance with this.

(*Lights fade, this time not to a complete blackout.*

Dim, amber light. Unreal atmosphere.

The GHOST *moves as before.*

*The other actors are confused and do not know where
to go.)*

BEST BOYD (*looking up at the theater lighting system*). Why isn't the scene changing this time?

DAWN. Unreality must be affecting the underlying structure of the play. I don't think this was supposed to happen.

GRIP. What is that thing? (*Indicates the* GHOST.)

DAWN (*glancing at* HUGH; *lowering her voice*). That's Hugh. From the future.

GRIP. That?

(DAWN *nods.*)

GRIP. Holy shit.

BEST BOYD. Things are just all screwed up aren't they?

DAWN. The whole temporal field is screwy. No telling which one of us is going to walk in here next.

GRIP. You mean we're all like that? In the future?

(*None of them had thought about that before.*

*They look at one another—the usual horror-movie
take.*

BLUE DONNA, *who has not been privy to this exchange,
walks over to the* GHOST, *who is still moving in rela-
tion to the bomb.*

She studies the GHOST *momentarily, then returns to the
others.*)

BLUE DONNA (*eyeing the* GHOST). I think it's all right now.

GRIP. What's all right?

BLUE DONNA. I don't think that thing will bother us for a while. I think we can start filming.

GRIP. You're out of your mind. We're getting on the goddamn boat, right now.

BLUE DONNA. We can't. It's not due here for a while.

GRIP. Then call it and get it here.

BLUE DONNA. I said we're going to start filming. Get to work.

GRIP. I think we should leave. Now.

BLUE DONNA (*ignoring* GRIP; *turning to* HUGH *and* JOE). You ready? All right, you remember the scene?

JOE LUBE COOL. We don't have to say nothing, right?

BLUE DONNA. No. No dialogue.

HUGH YOUNG. Is this after the butter scene?

BLUE DONNA. Yes.

HUGH YOUNG. So I already know him?

BLUE DONNA. Yes.

JOE LUBE COOL. Are we naked?

BLUE DONNA. Not completely. You get down to your straps. Then you take the straps off each other. Hugh, get out of that robe.

> (HUGH *and* JOE *do as instructed.*
>
> JOE *embraces and fondles* HUGH *with tenderness once they are ready.*
>
> *As soon as* JOE *embraces* HUGH *the first time,* MONTREAT *begins to stir.*
>
> *The others are all engaged in preparation for the taping and do not notice.*)

BLUE DONNA. All right. Dawn, you ready? (DAWN *is.*) All right. Here we go. The quicker we get this done, the quicker we get out of here. Boyd, you keep an eye on that thing back there. (*She means the* GHOST.) Got it? All right, when I say "Action," I want action. All right. Action.

> (MONTREAT *sits up and struggles to stand, holding his head as if it hurts.*

JOE *and* HUGH *have their backs to* MONTREAT, *but all*
the others see.)

GRIP. All right, that's it.

BLUE DONNA (*softly*). Don't turn around, Hugh. Just walk out this
way.

(MONTREAT *tries to say, "I just want to be in this scene,"*
but since he has shot the roof out of his mouth and
through the top of his head, he cannot speak clearly.)

HUGH YOUNG (*equally softly*). Go ahead and shoot the scene.

BLUE DONNA. That's not a good idea, Hugh.

HUGH YOUNG. Go ahead. It'll be all right.

(BLUE DONNA *hesitates.*

HUGH *reassures* JOE.)

DAWN. Are you sure?

HUGH YOUNG. Yes.

DAWN. You know Donna can't be liable.

HUGH YOUNG. I know. It doesn't matter. Go ahead.

(MONTREAT *has finally gotten to his feet.*
He is standing behind the blanket, just as he described
earlier.
The GHOST *is now moving very slowly but is still essen-*
tially as before.)

BLUE DONNA. All right. Everybody ready? (*Everybody is ready, even*
GRIP.) All right. Action.

(*They play out the scene in silence.*
The actors should relax and allow the audience to drink
in the tapestry.
HUGH *and* JOE *act out their love affair on the blanket.*
MONTREAT *watches as he had wished.*
DAWN *and* BLUE DONNA *capture the scene from two*
different angles.

GRIP *and* BEST BOYD *monitor the recording equipment.*

HUGH *and* JOE *should be as naked and as explicit or stylized as they wish.*

Use of the blanket and positioning of DAWN *and* BLUE DONNA *may soften the impact for the audience where necessary.*

The GHOST, *after a time and gradually, stops moving, puts on the robe, pulls up the hood, and approaches the area of the shoot.*

When the GHOST's *presence is noted, action ceases.*)

GHOST. You should leave now. Your boat will be here soon.

(*Exit* GHOST *as lights fade to black.*)

VOICEOVER. They looked each at the other. The cameras had ceased their efficient recording of light. The shutters had closed. The exposures had ceased to concern anyone. Somewhere on the film it was. Somewhere in those two black boxes, captured. They had forgotten what it was like not to be making the movie. They looked at each other. Like strangers. They packed away the equipment and moved it to the helicopter. They moved in complete efficiency and complete silence, as drained as if they had all had good sex with one another.

(*Lights rise slowly on the scene as the* VOICEOVER *describes it.*

Everyone is dismantling equipment except HUGH, JOE, *and* MONTREAT, *who are nowhere to be seen.*

No one speaks.

Everyone knows his or her assigned tasks.)

VOICEOVER. They knew they would never forget these past days. Any beach. Any time. They would remember the bomb and the noon sun over Bikini Atoll. Even years later, when *Big Bang* had long since become the underground classic porn film of its generation, even when its remarkable producer-director, Donna Morgan, would look back across her rich career to single out *Big Bang* as the most truly singular of her achievements. Dawn Stevens, from her eminent office on the crown of Wall Street, attorney to a condom magnate with international shipping interests, would sometimes tell stories about her madcap week on the beach when she was legal counsel to the notorious lesbian porno director who was obsessed with gay men. Even Grip recalled the experience with fondness afterward, until a freight truck struck his automobile on the interstate outside of Fresno a year or so later. Best Boyd, who had the foresight to provide Donna Morgan with a much-needed infusion of capital at a critical point in the postproduction of *Big Bang,* retired a millionaire following many other prudent investments. He was never again forced to carry heavy camera equipment across a windswept desolate beach in the South Pacific. As for Joe Lube Cool, his career as America's most beloved gay porno stud continued through many films and he was destined for crescendo after crescendo of acclaim. Most successful of all, of course, was the bomb, which changed the face of history and altered the destiny of nations.

> (*Enter* JOE LUBE COOL *and* HUGH YOUNG.
>
> HUGH *stands center stage, where his* GHOST *stood.*
>
> JOE *stands behind him, embracing him.*)

JOE LUBE COOL. I bet you look great in that scene.

> (*Pause; no answer from* HUGH.)

JOE LUBE COOL. Is something wrong?

HUGH YOUNG. No.

> (*Pause.*)

JOE LUBE COOL. You sure? You act like something's wrong.

HUGH YOUNG. I just wonder.

> (*Pause.*)

JOE LUBE COOL. Wonder what?

HUGH YOUNG. What's going to happen. Tomorrow.

JOE LUBE COOL. Things have been pretty crazy around here.

> (*Enter* MONTREAT, *not completely onto the playing area*
> *but into its perimeter, within sight of* HUGH YOUNG.
> *Enter* GHOST, *onto another part of the perimeter.*)

JOE LUBE COOL (*standing*). Is that the boat? (*Shouting.*) Hey! Hello out there! (*To* HUGH.) Hey, I've got to tell everybody, you want to wait here?

HUGH YOUNG. Don't go right now.

JOE LUBE COOL. What do you mean? There's the boat.

HUGH YOUNG. It's pretty far off.

JOE LUBE COOL (*looking horny again*). You got something in mind?

> (HUGH *stands and embraces* JOE.)

HUGH YOUNG. I don't want you to go right now, that's all.

JOE LUBE COOL. Look, I told you, you're going to be fine. You don't have anything to worry about.

> (*The lights are beginning to change as if at random.*)

HUGH YOUNG (*moving away from* JOE). All right.

JOE LUBE COOL (*moving toward the exit*). I'll be right back. You want to ride in the helicopter with me?

> (HUGH *does not answer.*
> *Exit* JOE.
> *Lights become dim but continue to shift.*)

HUGH YOUNG (*softly*). All right.

> (HUGH *turns to* MONTREAT *and the* GHOST.)

HUGH YOUNG (*to audience; awkwardly at first*). I'm not going on the boat. I guess you figured that. I'm tired. Really too tired. This whole business—I don't know. (*Pause.*) This place. I like the beach. I had a good time. I had a good time with Joe too. And I'm sorry about Pug. But. It's not my fault. I don't love Joe. I don't care who Joe loves. I don't. Anyway. I just don't want to go back, there's no reason to go. Things would just stay the same and I would think about this, all the time. The movies stink. I don't want to do it in the movies anymore. But why would I stop? (*Pause.*) I just wanted to say something. To you folks. I've been watching you the whole time. Just sitting there. I know you don't really exist but who cares? Even if you don't, I didn't want you to think I'm stuck up. (*Pause.*) There was something I really wanted to tell you. But I can't think of it. Right now.

    (*Watches the* GHOST.)

VOICEOVER. No one knows what happened to the mysterious beauty whose performance in *Big Bang* was his third, his last, and his finest. When the others returned to the beach, he had vanished. The search, as he had guessed, went quickly, since the searchers could not afford to keep the boat waiting. The boat, a fishing trawler aptly named the *Lucky Dragon*, sailed south, as Blue Donna had known it would.

    (*The* GHOST OF HUGH YOUNG *brings the book to* HUGH
        YOUNG.

    They join MONTREAT.

    HUGH *gives the inevitable last look, as if, of course, he*
        had known this was coming.

    He sets the book onstage in a conspicuous place.)

In the morning, at dawn, from the deck of the boat they saw the flash of light and felt the shock of the bomb. By then the

Lucky Dragon had sailed far to the south. They did not see, for no one was there to see, Hugh Young in the twilight before dawn, waiting in shades on the sand near the bomb's tower, wanting to see the whole thing up close for himself.

(*Blackout.*)